ARCHITECTURE 3s

TWENTIETH-CENTURY HOUSES

Introduction by Beth Dunlop and Denis Hector

Each house in this book represents a high point – and, in the case of Fallingwater, perhaps *the* high point – of the *œuvre* of their designers. They are grandly sited or grandly executed, sometimes both, and they each invite examination into the relationship not just between architecture and nature but between man and nature.

Certainly each of these three houses – Fallingwater by Frank Lloyd Wright, Alvar Aalto's Villa Mairea, and the Eames House by Charles and Ray Eames (or Case Study House #8 as it was officially, if not universally called) – has a remarkable setting. Indeed, Fallingwater is perhaps one of the most famously sited buildings ever designed and in this respect it shares a certain bravado with the Eames house. If Fallingwater seems to perch precariously atop boulders as the water rushes past, the Eames House has its own astonishing berth against a ridge, at the edge of a cliff looking out over the Pacific Ocean. By contrast the Villa Mairea sits in a clearing in the woods in which the land falls away gently rather than precipitously. It is not a comparably dramatic site, yet with its curvilinear forms contained within an orthogonal context, it is nonetheless architecture primarily concerned with nature.

At first glance, these might seem to be three quite dissimilar houses: Fallingwater with its powerful slabs of concrete, Villa Mairea with its interior forest of wooden poles akin to the birch trees in the forest beyond, the Eames House with its collage-like assemblage of steel and glass. Yet each building embodies a level of experimentation – from the precariously cantilevered slabs of Fallingwater, to the subtle interior spaces of the Villa Mairea, to the Eames House, which was of course intentionally experimental as part of the much larger California Case Study House venture. But for none of these houses was it experimentation for its own sake; rather an exploration, a venture that pushed its architect to new levels of both perception and intelligence.

This remains true to this day. Each of these houses offer a level of wisdom and insight that, in many ways, demonstrate any number of architectural issues. Indeed, one can trace a short and partial history of architecture by simply moving from Fallingwater (completed in 1935) to the Eames House (completed in 1949). In the former, structure reigns triumphant – the house is in many ways the culmination of a near century of architectural endeavour. But in the latter, structural acumen is a given, and the preoccupation is no longer structural but concerned with production, or, in fact, mass production; the linking of architecture to the building industry.

Each house was also romantic in a very different way. Wright's work certainly sprang from his readings and rereadings of architectural movements and impulses, while Aalto took Modernism and through it reinterpreted the Finnish vernacular. Charles and Ray Eames, a husband and wife team, were often regarded as sentimentalists within the Modern Movement, not because their architecture lacked the discipline or rigour of the International Style, but because of their attachment to things – their idiosyncratic personal collections – and their ability to incorporate it into a greater collage of work.

Both Fallingwater and Villa Mairea were built before the Second World War, and thus they embody a luxurious, more grandiose approach to Modernism than the work of the immediate postwar era. The sumptuousness of much prewar architecture was eclipsed by the ugliness and the horror of the war. Thus the Eames House strips away much of that former extravagance – at least in the structure itself, not in the finish and furnishings – in the interest of an architecture that could go from the elite to the masses. The war had sobered the world, and architects and builders of houses were not immune to this. If the prewar era offered an environment to integrate architecture and nature and somehow enhance both, the postwar climate led to a more temperate set of inquiries.

The legacy of these three designers and their houses has been a powerful one, although in varying degrees. Wright was, of course, the dominant figure of American architecture for the better part of a century and is still celebrated today. He produced generations of followers who, to this day, work in the splendid desert atelier setting of Taliesin West in Arizona. For several decades now, Charles and Ray Eames have been associated with an icon of residential design, if more for a single chair design than anything else. The same avid discipleship perhaps never came Aalto's way within his lifetime; indeed he was perhaps more enigmatic and harder to penetrate – much less to emulate – even though the centenary of his birth in 1998 provoked widespread interest in his work.

As Robert McCarter points out, despite a prodigious early career, the Great Depression had effected Wright along with the rest of the country. In 1935, Edgar S. Kaufmann commissioned Wright – then sixty-eight years old – to design Fallingwater, and provided Wright with the opportunity to re-emerge, and even reinvent himself. And of course, since it was Wright, he did it with his own personal brand of architectural flamboyance. The drawings alone, of the vast cantilevered slabs hovering over the vast rocks and rushing water, are enough to take one's breath away.

Fallingwater did not break with past work, nor did it embrace new movements in architecture, rather it is a momentary culmination of Wright's work and ideas. Few houses embody an architect's work and ideas as singularly as Fallingwater; the architect himself has said that its roots are easily found in the Barnsdall House, built in 1921 in Los Angeles, and in many of his earliest structures in Oak Park, Illinois. In his *Modern Architecture*, the architectural historian Vincent Scully points out that in

Fallingwater, Wright 'welded together almost everything that had gone before: his early work and its continuous space with Mayan pyramidal massing, structural continuity in reinforced concrete with neo-plasticism, the thin machined screen of metal and glass with the asymmetry and nature-worship of romantic-naturalism and the geometric clarity of romantic-classic form.'

The site, a waterfall in fast-moving Bear Run, a tributary creek of the Youghiogheny River in Western Pennsylvania, was a piece of land that had previously been in use as a weekend house by Edgar and Lillian Kaufmann, after two decades as a summer and weekend camp for employees of the family's department store. The design process continued throughout construction, and typically Wright ignored engineers' reports and went ahead with his own ambitious cantilevering and projecting of concrete slabs. Although the plan is actually fairly simple, it seems to be the reverse when actually experienced, in fact its spatial texture is incredibly complex.

Fallingwater is a house of primal power, and yet one that turns out to be softer and better environmentally adapted to the weathered characteristics of the site than the widely published drawings and texts about it might imply. This is due in part to the at once simple, and yet utterly complex, relationship of the house with nature, which architect Charles Moore, in Reyner Banham's *Architecture of the Four Ecologies*, described as an 'intimate involvement with the site, capturing and intensifying the natural ledging of rock and cave with the defiant thrust of human movement, with smooth concrete bridges, crossing the crevice, darting up the hill, and balancing out over the falling stream … The house itself is a place to be explored as fully as the forested and craggy site which it has extended.'

The latter statement might just as easily be applied to Aalto's Villa Mairea, a summer home in Noormarkku. Unlike Fallingwater and the Eames House, its siting is subtle, without dramatic topography or views. Experiencing the house is not unlike experiencing nature, and this is what it is primarily concerned with, more so than specific site or context.

The owners of the house, Harry and Mairea Gullichsen, were founders of a Helsinki art gallery, which after some permutations became Artek, still a renowned manufacturer and distributor of, among other things, Aalto's furniture and glass art objects. Mairea Gullichsen, an heiress to a large timber, paper and cellulose fortune, had studied painting in Paris and thus shared a number of Aalto's interests. She gave him a comparatively free hand in the design of the house and from the start, in fact, she encouraged him to explore new ideas and to strive for new insights.

Aalto began the house toward the end of 1937, and in its early incarnations it was highly influenced by the recently completed Fallingwater: early plans show cantilevered balconies and an undulating basement storey, and, although the final house is most unlike Fallingwater it is still easy to see the Wrightian influence. In a way, both houses belong to what might best be called the romantic and expressionistic wing of the Modern Movement, which itself is heir to the Arts and Crafts Movement. And be it direct lineage or merely the influence of mutual interest, there is a connection between the two which is expressed in Villa Mairea. Part modern, part Arts and Crafts, part Finnish vernacular, it is a handmade house and completely situational – so much so that the design was changed after the foundation was finished, when Aalto had second thoughts about it. The completed house is no less accomplished for the change and still has the sense of being refined on site – a kind of spontaneity of form. The house's kinship with Finnish National Romanticism and, more indirectly, its relationship with the Arts and Crafts Movement has caused it to fall outside of the critical dialogue surrounding the Modern Movement.

Aalto is set apart from his contemporary architects. In *Essays in Architectural Criticism: Modern Architecture and Historical Change*, historian Alan Colquhoun points out that his forms absorb meanings from 'the context rather than pre-ordained categories. Aalto's strength lay in his ability to maintain artistic control over many contradictory elements and an apparent excess of ideas, which he was able to synthesize into a rich metonymy of architectural forms.'

If Aalto was set apart, Charles and Ray Eames were in the thick of the postwar modernist movement. Both were Cranbrook-educated (Charles in a class that included Edmund Bacon, Harry Weese, Harry Bertoia and Ralph Rapson), and were thus friends and colleagues of Eero Saarinen, among many others. The house they built for themselves came about not as an individual effort but a collegial one – part of a movement. The house was built as part of the Case Study House initiative, a project sponsored by *Arts & Architecture* magazine to foster an understanding of technological breakthroughs in construction and promote prefabrication and mass production. The years after the Second World War saw hundreds of American soldiers returning from the battlefields in need of housing, a problem for which the burgeoning Modern Movement was beginning to provide solutions. Thus the house was intended to be an example of what critic Charles Jencks has called the 'social use of technology', which is indeed what separates the Case Study houses from their forebears: they were studies in the structural use of technology for architectural, even artistic, purposes but they were not really intended for social purposes – at least in comparison with the fervent idealism of much prewar architecture.

The Eames House was publicly previewed in an announcement in *Arts & Architecture* in December 1945, which read as follows: 'This is ground in meadow and hill, protected on all sides from intrusive developments free of the usual surrounding clutter, safe from urban clatter; not, however, removed from the necessary conveniences and the reassurances of city living … This house – in its free relation [to] the ground, the trees, the sea – with constant proximity to the whole vast order of nature acts as re-orientor and "shock absorber"'.

Fallingwater was built midstream; Villa Mairea was tucked into a glade; the Eames House was not so secluded. Rather the Eames House was a big-view site, three acres along the Pacific Palisades, as part of the acreage bought by John Entenza for *Arts & Architecture*. Unlike both Fallingwater and Villa Mairea, it was not intended as a summer or country house – as a full-time residence and studio, it had to meet very different considerations. As a steel building, it is more volumetric than architectonic, and, significantly, is the only one of the three to be designed in the International Style, which is to say that it is not just a modernist house, but a modernist house in the genealogical camp of the Bauhaus. Yet, like both Fallingwater and Villa Mairea (and to the dismay of the more orthodox proponents of the International Style), there was a spontaneity to the design. In *Blueprints for Modern Living: History and Legacy of the Case Study Houses*, Charles Moore termed this 'the general Eames approach, experimental, hands-on, improvisatory, quirky, was a much-needed antidote to the cut-and-dried recipes of routine Modernism then being taught in the schools.'

In some ways, the Eames House has the character of an exhibition space. With its double-height living space and room divisions that became showcases for art, what Moore called 'the wonderful things from everywhere', it recalls Le Corbusier's Pavillon de l'Esprit Nouveau, built for the Exposition Internationale des Arts Décoratifs in Paris, 1925. To be sure, the house, as Reyner Banham wrote, 'reinforced the dogmas of honesty, clarity and unity, the exposure of structure, the use of certifiably modern materials and the absence of ornament', but it is also as much personal as it is universal. It was this personal quality, the housing of the Eames' own collections, which made the house controversial. In his essay 'The Wit of Technology' of 1966, Michael Brawne pointed out that the house parted from its 'nearest' predecessors because its composition was 'wholly additive, with frame and cladding not separated but working together.' However, Brawne continued, the house possessed 'wit, a quality extremely rare in architecture. Its wit is, of course, largely the result of the additive process, of the seemingly casual juxtaposition of different elements.'

Frank Lloyd Wright
Fallingwater
Bear Run, Pennsylvania 1935

Robert McCarter

Photography
Peter Cook; cover detail
supplied by VIEW, photograph
also by Peter Cook
Drawings
Robert Blatter, James Buzbee,
John Hewitt

1 Frank Lloyd Wright, photograph taken during the period in which Fallingwater was designed and built.
2 Frederick Robie House, Chicago, Illinois, 1909.
3 Taliesin, Frank Lloyd Wright's own home and studio, built in Spring Green, Wisconsin, 1911; rebuilt 1915 and 1925.
4 Richard Lloyd Jones house, Tulsa, Oklahoma, 1929, perspective drawing.
5 Taliesin, stone walls and gate.
6 Edgar and Lillian Kaufmann on the bedroom terrace at Fallingwater in the 1940s.

Fallingwater, as Frank Lloyd Wright named the house he designed for Edgar and Lillian Kaufmann in 1935, is without question the most famous modern house in the world. Over 75,000 people visit the house every year, despite its remote site deep in the woods on Bear Run, a mountain stream in southwestern Pennsylvania, and it has been named the best American building of the last 125 years by the American Institute of Architects. While numerous books and articles have been written on Fallingwater, it has rarely been discussed as an experience, a place that we inhabit. Scholarly studies tend to search for new historical information rather than focusing on what is there for all visitors to see, if they only know what to look for; this text will attempt to break the prevailing silence about the spatial experience of Fallingwater, particularly of its interior. Constructive criticism is the result of a powerful, transformative experience, the quality of which we seek to communicate to others, hoping they will also feel compelled to undergo the same experience. As George Steiner said, 'In this attempt at persuasion originate the truest insights criticism can afford'.[1] This book is intended to encourage the desire to inhabit and experience this outstanding house by analyzing Wright's conception and development of the design, reviewing critical aspects of the construction process which brought the house into being, summarizing the exceptional qualities of the house by walking the reader through its site and its spaces, and briefly examining the importance of Fallingwater as a work of architecture.

The design of Fallingwater

In 1935, at the end of the Great Depression in America, Frank Lloyd Wright was already 68 years old. In the 43 years since starting his own practice in 1892, Wright had built hundreds of works, including the famous buildings of his Prairie Period such as the Robie House, the Martin House, the Dana House, the Coonley House, Unity Temple and the Larkin Building. He had left Chicago and its influential suburb, Oak Park, in 1911, retreating to the remote valley owned by his mother's relatives near Madison, Wisconsin, where he had built Taliesin, his home and studio. Here, at the age of 45, he had begun what many considered to be his second career with such works as the Midway Gardens, the Hollyhock House, the Imperial Hotel in Tokyo and the California concrete block houses for Millard, Ennis, Storer and Freeman, to name only the most famous. It was altogether a long and prodigious career by any reckoning, and one unmatched in America before or since. Wright's practice had all but disappeared in the economic decline of the late 1920s, his last built work being a house for his cousin Richard Lloyd Jones in 1929. He had written his autobiography during those slow years, summing up his seminal contributions to the development of an American architecture. So it should not be surprising that, by 1935, most people in America assumed that Wright had retired from practice, happy to bask in the glory of the new architectural histories that portrayed him as the grandfather of the modern architecture being built around the world. Joseph Connors notes that, given Wright's age, it seemed evident that, as these histories implied, 'he had pointed the way to the promised land that he would never himself enter'.[2]

4

It had never been wise to count Wright out, however; throughout his life he had repeatedly rebounded from a variety of personal and professional calamities, and was about to do so once again. As we might have guessed, given his extraordinary energy and creativity, Wright had not been idle during these years of professional inactivity; nor did he consider himself 'finished' as an architect. Even though he was then approaching 70, he would live to the age of 92, building hundreds of buildings in the next 25 years – his third career as an architect. Pivotal in this resurgence was Wright's marriage in 1928 to Oglivanna Lazovich, born in Montenegro and a follower of the Russian mystic Georgei Gurdjieff. When Wright founded the Taliesin Fellowship in 1932, offering apprenticeships to interested young students willing to work on the farm and in the drafting room, he to a large degree modelled this enterprise – with Oglivanna's guidance – on Gurdjieff's Institute in Fontainebleau; yet it was also related to Ashbee's Arts and Crafts colony near London, Hubbard's Roycrofters in East Aurora, as well as such American utopian experiments as Brook Farm, the Oneida Community, and New Harmony.[3] Opened in the very depths of the Great Depression, the Fellowship succeeded largely because of Wright's continued reputation as the greatest American architect; students enrolled from all over the country and the world, coming to Spring Green, Wisconsin, helping to rebuild the dilapidated buildings of Taliesin and the Hillside Home School, which Wright had built for his aunts in 1902, and which he now converted into the drafting room for the Taliesin Fellowship. The students received no pay for their work in construction, farming, cooking, cleaning and drafting at Taliesin – in fact, they paid Wright for the privilege.

5

One of the apprentices who joined the Fellowship in October 1934 was Edgar Kaufmann, Jr, a young art student whose father was Edgar Kaufmann, owner of the Kaufmann's Store in Pittsburgh. In 1871 the senior Kaufmann's father had been one of the founders of the Kaufmann's Store, a successful retail business offering ready-made men's clothing, which, by the time Edgar Kaufmann assumed control of the business in 1913, had become one of the largest department stores of its kind in the country. At the end of 1934, the Kaufmanns visited their son at Taliesin, and Wright was invited to Pittsburgh to discuss several projects, one of which was a country house to replace a rudimentary cottage that the family had used for over a decade; it was then that Wright first visited the site.[4] Bear Run, the stream over which the house is placed, was typical and unexceptional before it became the site for Fallingwater. Like many Appalachian mountain streams fed by springs in this area of Pennsylvania, it would never have attracted attention had it not been bought in 1933 by Edgar and Lillian Kaufmann as a site for their weekend house. In 1913, the year Kaufmann took over management of the family business, the store leased the Bear Run property for use by the employees as a summer and weekend camp; it had been similarly used since 1890 by the Masons, and there were 15 structures, including a clubhouse, a small train station, several cottages and a dance pavilion already existing on a 1,635 acre site.[5] In 1921, Kaufmann and his wife built a modest cabin on Bear Run, 1,500 feet southeast of the falls. With its screened sleeping porches

6

7 Wright and the Taliesin Fellowship apprentices, 1937. To the right are the two apprentices involved in overseeing construction of Fallingwater, Bob Mosher and Edgar Tafel; to the left of Mosher (with arms on desk) is William Wesley Peters, who developed the concrete cantilevered structural floors for Fallingwater.

8 Edgar Kaufmann's office at the Kaufmann's Store in Pittsburgh, designed by Wright.

9 Porter cottage and bridge existing on the Bear Run site prior to the construction of Fallingwater. The bridge is in the exact location of the bridge later built by Wright; the cottage occupies the site of the future guest house; and the main house would be located to the left, in front of the existing entry drive.

10 Fallingwater, view of the site before its construction, as seen from below the waterfall; photograph taken c1900.

11 Topographic site survey given to Wright by Edgar Kaufmann in March 1935. Note that the centre of the drawing – clearly intended by Kaufmann to be the building site for the house – is below and to the south of the waterfalls. Wright placed Fallingwater above and to the north of the falls, ensuring a southern orientation for the house.

7

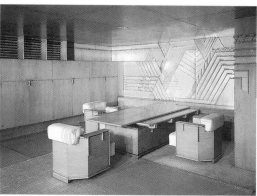

8

9

and lack of plumbing, heating and electricity, it allowed the urbane Kaufmanns a true retreat from city life. The store employee's association bought the Bear Run property in 1926, with Kaufmann holding the mortgage; in 1933 the Kaufmanns assumed personal ownership of the original property, and were eventually to add to it until the property included 1,914 acres, enough to protect and conserve the watershed of Bear Run.

Wright returned to Taliesin and was sent a site survey in March of the following year, showing the stream, contours, major trees and boulders. Nine months went by after Wright's visit to the site with no discernable evidence that he was thinking of a design for the Kaufmann House; yet, in writing of his own design process a few years before, Wright had stated that one should 'conceive the building in the imagination, not on paper but in the mind, thoroughly – before touching paper. Let it live there – gradually taking more definite form before committing it to the draughting board. When the thing lives for you – start to plan it with tools. Not before ... It is best to cultivate the imagination to construct and complete the building before working on it with T-square and triangle'.[6] Not very helpful advice for most mortals, but it appears that Wright followed this method in his initial design for the Kaufmann House. Various apprentices have conflicting memories, but Bob Mosher and Edgar Tafel, both of whom would serve as on-site supervising apprentices during Fallingwater's construction, tell the same story of Wright receiving a call from Kaufmann one Sunday morning in late September, saying to Kaufmann, 'Come along, E J, we're ready for you'.[7] Kaufmann was leaving Milwaukee for Taliesin, a mere two-hour drive, and not a single drawing had been made! The understandable panic of the apprentices did not disturb Wright as he set about drawing first the three floor plans, working on top of the site survey and using different coloured pencils for each floor, next a north–south section through the house, and finally a south elevation from across the stream. Donald Hoffmann has written, 'His sketches may have looked a little rough to Kaufmann [who had no idea they had just been drawn], but they turned out to be a remarkably complete presentation of the house as it would be built: the house had been conceived with an awesome finality'.[8]

Kaufmann arrived, and was presented with the design, which he approved, despite its being in a different location on the site than he had apparently imagined. The area selected to be surveyed on the site map suggests that Kaufmann expected the house to be built to the south of the stream, looking at the falls from below.[9] Kaufmann was in fact surprised that the house was to be built above the falls, but Wright had no intention either of having the house face north, an inappropriate orientation for the sun, or to have the waterfall present merely as an image to be looked at from the house. He told Kaufmann, 'I want you to live with the waterfall, not just to look at it, but for it to become an integral part of your lives'.[10] Wright pointed out the critical difference between hearing the waterfall (an intimate, nearer experience) and simply looking at it (a formal, distant experience) when he later described the design, saying of Kaufmann, 'He loved the site where the house was built and liked to listen to the waterfall. So that was the prime motive of the design. I think you can hear the waterfall when you look at the design. At least it is there, and he lives intimately with the thing he loves'.[11]

In laying out these early sketch-plans, Wright had oriented the site map so that the existing roadway cutting across the face of the hill above the falls was horizontal, as was the waterfall itself; the house was laid out at a 60-degree angle to the road and falls. The three main concrete piers, which were the first things Wright drew, were set perpendicular to the stream, parallel to the existing bridge, so that the house faced 30 degrees east of due south. This provided for the dynamic diagonal views of the house both from the entry drive and from the flat rock ledge below the falls. As Connors put it: 'Thus if the house was photogenic it was not by accident. The picturesque view from the boulder downstream ... was built into the design from the start, and to make sure the visitor took it in, a set of stairs was cut into the riverbank leading down to the chosen viewpoint'.[12] These diagonal views were documented in a series of perspective drawings completed soon after Kaufmann's visit,[13] including the famous drawing

10

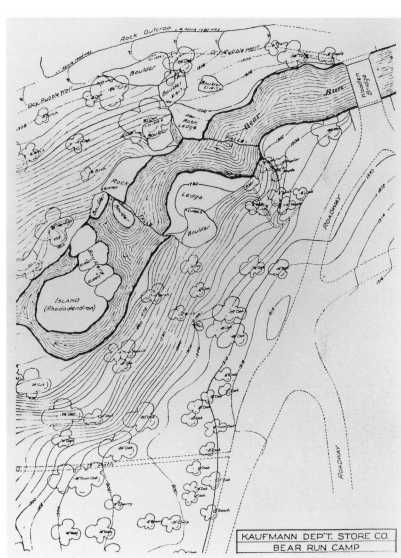

11

12 Fallingwater, sketch perspective, as seen from below the waterfall.
13 Fallingwater, sketch perspective from hillside across stream.
14 Fallingwater, final perspective rendering from below waterfall. This drawing appeared on the wall behind Wright in the cover photograph of *Time* magazine, 17 January 1938.

15 Samuel Freeman House, Los Angeles, California, 1923. Mitred glass corners with no vertical mullions.
16 Mrs Thomas Gale House, Chicago, Illinois, designed 1904, built 1909. 30 years later, Wright had trellises similar to those at Fallingwater added to this drawing (at the far left), and stated that this house was the 'progenitor as to general type' for Fallingwater.

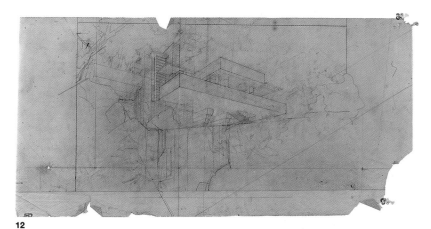

12

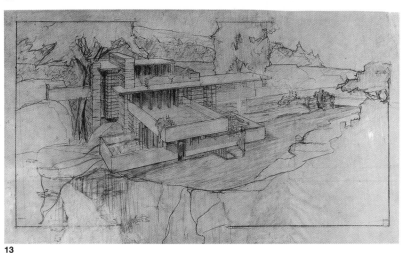

13

by Wright's own hand of the view from below the waterfall. This beautiful perspective, done with colour pencils, appeared in the background when Wright's photograph appeared on the cover of the January 17, 1938 issue of *Time* magazine, in which he was profiled and the house introduced to the country.

Historians have often claimed that the design for Fallingwater, with its smooth rectangular concrete planes interlocking and cantilevering out into space, was in some way Wright's 'answer' to the International Style of architecture that had been canonized in the 1932 Museum of Modern Art exhibition. But an examination of Wright's earlier work, and the close relation of Fallingwater to it, indicates this to be an invention on the part of the historians. Wright was quite specific about this, saying of Fallingwater: 'The ideas involved here are in no wise changed from those of early work. The materials and methods of construction come through them ... The effects you see in this house are not superficial effects, and are entirely consistent with the Prairie Houses of 1901–10'.[14] In briefly analyzing the sources for Fallingwater evident in Wright's own earlier work, we will find that the lack of preliminary sketch studies in his design process was possible due to the fact that he designed buildings in sequence, as variations on a common theme – spatial, constructional or site-specific. These sequential designs can be treated as the preliminary studies for Fallingwater, part of what Wright called the 'constantly accumulating residue of formula'[15] that he achieved by designing each building not as a single unique form but as part of the development of spatial types, perfected through a series of designs for different buildings.

Wright himself stated that the house for Mrs Thomas Gale, designed in 1904 and built in Oak Park in 1909, was the 'progenitor as to general type' for Fallingwater, and he had his apprentice John Howe add a roof trellis similar to those at Fallingwater to the original perspective for the Gale House, even though this detail did not exist on either the working drawings or the house as built.[16] Even without this detail, the Gale House develops a number of elements that would later be used in the design for Fallingwater. Despite having a simple rectangular plan, when seen from the front the house appears to be a series of horizontal planes and balconies projecting from a core of vertical slab-like walls, with only continuous window bands separating the horizontal elements. Finished in stucco plaster, its exterior has a similar texture to concrete, and, like Fallingwater, the Gale House is designed to take maximum advantage of a diagonal view. The primary cantilever of the balcony that runs along the stream at Fallingwater finds its precedent in the Frederick Robie House, built in Chicago in 1909; the enormous cantilever of the main roof is complemented by a series of crossing trajectories at second floor level and in the brick piers and walls below, and the whole is adjusted to attain the greatest impact in the diagonal perspective view from the street corner.[17] The rustic, beautifully-set stonework of Fallingwater was first employed by Wright in his own home, Taliesin, built in Spring Green in 1911, where he also contrasted it to the smooth golden plasterwork inside and out. The open glass corner, with the horizontal steel mullions passing around the corner and the vertical joint unframed, which runs up three storeys through the kitchen and small bedrooms at Fallingwater, was initially built out in the Samuel Freeman House of 1923 in Los Angeles, and later in the Richard Lloyd Jones House of Tulsa, Oklahoma in 1929. Fallingwater's balconies cantilevering all around from a central structural core are seen in the Malcolm Willey House project of 1932, and their structural interpretation in reinforced concrete appears earlier in projects for the Elizabeth Noble Apartment Building and the St Mark's Tower, both of 1929. Finally, despite its differing countenance on the exterior, the plan of Fallingwater was developed, as Wright said, from those of the Prairie Houses; the basic organization of a cruciform interpenetrating a square is to be found here, as is the typical asymmetrical, spiralling, perimeter movement pattern and hidden entry.[18]

The plan of Fallingwater, first emerging in the drawings done while Kaufmann made his way to Taliesin that Sunday morning, emphasizes the underlying order of the series of parallel walls and piers, standing on the rock ledge perpendicular to the stream on its north shore, which support the main volume of the house.

14

15

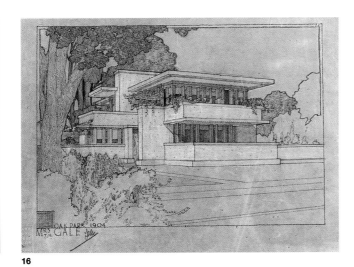

16

17

17 Malcolm Willey House
project, first scheme, 1932.
Balconied terraces
cantilevered all around
a central masonry core.
18 Elizabeth Noble Apartment
Building project, 1929.
Reinforced concrete
cantilevered
terraces projecting through
vertical glazing.
19 St Mark's Apartment Tower
project, 1929. Reinforced
concrete floors cantilevered from
central vertical mast or core
structure.

20 Fallingwater, sketch plan,
first version, September 1935,
with all three floors represented
(each by a different coloured
pencil) and superimposed. This
is one of the drawings Wright
executed while Kaufmann drove
the two hours from Milwaukee
to Taliesin.
21 Fallingwater, sketch plan
with section, second version,
first – or main – floor.

These are located on five equally-spaced lines that are struck across the drawing, creating four bays defining, starting from the east or entry side: the loggia
and east terrace; the entry, library and stair down to the stream; and the living-
dining room. A fifth equal bay, not defined by Wright in the same way as the others on any of the early drawings (by a line struck across the plan), defines the
kitchen behind and the edge of the balcony overlooking the waterfall. In the
main floor plan, the pier lying under the centre of the living room is not matched,
as the others are, by a square stone pier or wall rising through the living room to
support the floors above; only the dining table's central position marks this hidden support below. Though Wright's initial plan suggests that the house's 'centre of gravity' would be along the east edge of the living room, where the two
stairs begin their ascent and descent, the two piers, fireplace and entry wall of
the living room create a square central volume, off the corners of which open the
entry, stairs, kitchen and balconies. This 'great room' contains in a single volume
almost all the rooms – living, dining, library and entry – typically found in the first
floor of Wright's Prairie Houses; only the kitchen remains outside. In those early
houses, Wright's overall symmetrical order in plan allowed the corners to open;
here the open corner becomes such a strong spatial element in its own right that
it allows the plan to do without literal symmetry. The house is held together by
the diagonal tensions between intimate internal places, so that the outer edges
are free to respond to the natural site, as when the rear wall of the house steps
along the drive in response to the natural rock wall of the hill behind.

The construction of Fallingwater
As with all of Wright's buildings, the designing did not stop at the start of construction. Of particular interest are Wright's many statements about how much
he learned from the contractor and construction workers on his jobs, and how
often this new knowledge allowed him to change and improve the design during
construction. At other times he saw in the rising forms new spatial opportunities
that had not been apparent during design even to his imaginative inner eye,
requiring changes that included the removal and reconstruction of parts of the
building already completed.[19] This necessitated Wright's regular presence on
the construction site, which had been the rule during the earlier phases of his
career. However, with the rapid nationwide expansion of his practice during the
period of Fallingwater's construction – the Johnson Wax Buildings in Wisconsin,
his own projects in Arizona, the campus for Florida Southern College, and the
Usonian Houses being built from east to west coast – Wright relied more and
more on his Taliesin apprentices to undertake construction supervision. While
Wright had an astonishingly accurate intuitive sense of materials and their constructional and structural possibilities, he was often unable to pass this on to his
apprentices; Wright's judgements made on the construction site were inevitably
and unnervingly correct, but his dictates from afar were noticeably less so.[20]
However, not following exactly the drawings done under Wright's supervision at
Taliesin, or allowing the contractor to make changes not first specifically
approved by Wright – even if they seemed clearly called for – would, if discov-

18

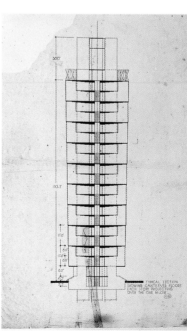

19

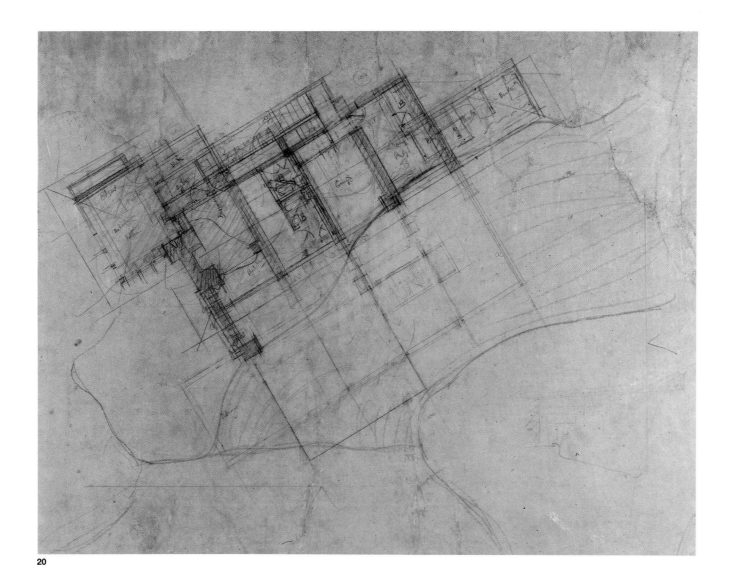

20

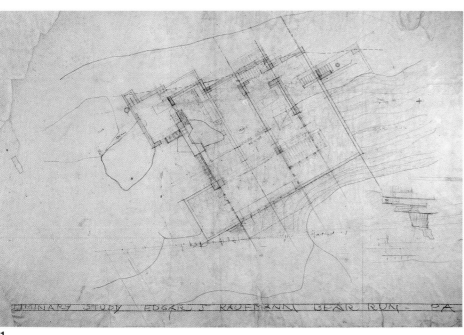

21

ered by Wright, result in the apprentice being recalled to Taliesin and replaced by another. Wright's apprentices were thus in a no-win situation when alone and facing a dilemma on the construction site, with predictable results.

Preliminary plans had been sent to Kaufmann on October 15, 1935, and after visiting the site again Wright told him to assume that the minimum cost for the house and its furnishings would be $35,000; he gave no maximum, and Fallingwater finally cost $75,000 for initial construction, $22,000 for completion and furnishing. The guest house, garage and servants' quarters added in 1939 cost an additional $50,000. Towards the end of 1935, an old rock quarry was opened about 500 feet west of the waterfall, and Kaufmann wrote to Wright that 'they are taking the strata of the stone as it comes and breaking it up in pieces about 12 inches to 14 inches wide and 24 inches long, the thickness being the strata of the quarry'.[21] Final plans followed in March, and Kaufmann reported that he was having a sample wall built; he did not tell Wright he was having the plans reviewed by his consulting engineers, who from the very start were doubtful about both Wright's competence with a material like reinforced concrete, still considered 'new' in America and untried in domestic construction, and Wright's decision to place the house on the rock ledge over the waterfall. The reviews were sent to Wright, who immediately told Kaufmann to return the drawings to Taliesin, 'since he did not deserve the house'. Kaufmann apologized and gave his approval for the working drawings – he later had the engineers' reports buried in the stone wall near the dining table.[22] Wright visited the site in April, approving the stonework in the sample wall, but in early June he rejected both the stonework and the concrete on the bridge, which had to be completely rebuilt. As the construction progressed, Kaufmann suggested a number of small but important changes and additions to the design, the first of which was the plunge pool to the north of the shallow stream, which had not been in the original plans. The Taliesin apprentice Bob Mosher was assigned by Wright to live on the site and supervise the construction, and in addition he sent Wright specific measurements to help with incorporating those of Kaufmann's proposals with which Wright agreed.

By the first week of August the formwork was being built for the concrete slab of the first floor with its extended cantilevers; Wright had ignored the engineers' recommendation that the pier-walls supporting this floor be three feet in width rather than two feet, as he had designed them. Wright had absolute confidence in his own structural intuition as well as that of his chief associates in this area: Mendel Glickman, an older structural engineer with the Fellowship, and William Wesley Peters, a brilliant, largely self-taught structural thinker who remained all his life with Wright at Taliesin. Peters and Glickman were responsible for calculating the structural loads in the revolutionary, thin-shell, reinforced concrete, hollow 'mushroom' columns that Wright sketched intuitively for the Johnson Wax Building in 1937, which held five times their design loads, and at Fallingwater they calculated the loads in the reinforced concrete, double-cantilevered slab with integral upturned beams that supported the flagstone floor – an upside-down early version of the 'waffle' slab capable of the 18 foot cantilevers out over the stream. This ingenious design placed the flat slab on the bottom, forming the ceiling of the space below; as the flagstone floor conceals from above the space inside this structural slab, only by studying the section drawing can we discern the integral beams that, with the balcony walls at the edge, do the real structural work in this floor.

The most serious mistake in the construction of Fallingwater was made by the contractor, engineer and Kaufmann in the pouring of this first floor slab on 19 August; at Kaufmann's request the engineers had redrawn Wright's reinforcing plan for the slab, and by their own admission, 'put in twice as much steel as was called for on [Wright's] plans'.[23] This excess steel not only added enormous weight to the carefully calculated slab, but was set so close together that the concrete often did not properly fill in between the reinforcing bars, causing an actual loss of strength. In building the wooden formwork to hold the concrete while it was setting, the contractor also neglected to build in a slight upward curve or 'camber', to compensate for the structurally insignificant and normal

22 Fallingwater, axonometric (redrawn) showing Wright's ingenious 'waffle' slab design.
23 Detail section and elevation of living room, looking east towards entry. Stone stairs going up at left, suspended stairs at 'hatch' going down to stream at right.

24 Preliminary section. Initial design indicates boulder at living room to be cut off flat, flush with floor.

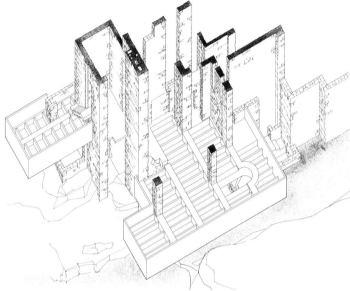

22

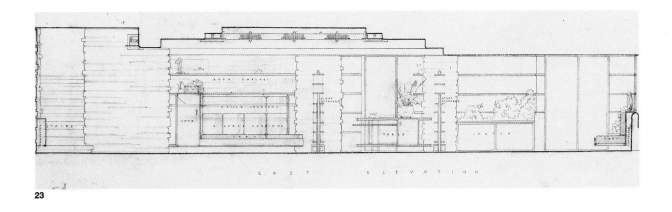

23

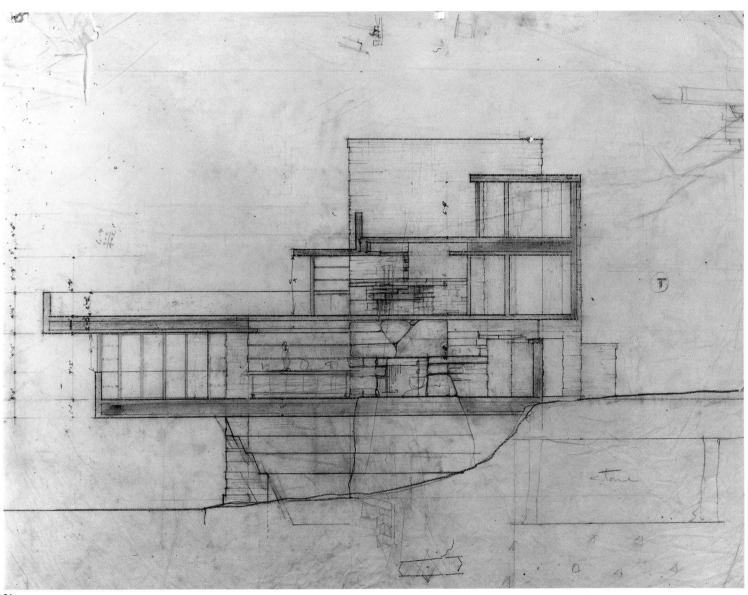

24

slight settling that occurs over time in reinforced concrete that spans or cantilevers. The result of these blunders, of which Wright was unaware at the time, are the drooping lines of the main cantilever and the cracks in the concrete that have plagued the house since its completion. That Wright's initial design, refined by Glickman and Peters, has been easily able to sustain these added structural loads and construction weaknesses, argues convincingly for the quality of their structural intuition. By early September, Wright found out about the extra steel in the first floor slab and called Mosher back to Taliesin in disgrace; Wright replaced him with the apprentice Edgar Tafel, but Mosher was later to return to Fallingwater.

Despite their complicity in the gravest error made during Fallingwater's construction, the consulting engineers continued to cast doubt upon the structural viability of the house even as construction proceeded. When Wright extended the west terrace out to 28 feet in length, the engineers recommended that a stone wall be added under the principal beam to reduce its span from 16 to eight feet. During the test-loading of this terrace, Wright discovered the added wall; 'No one had asked him about the wall, so he did not tell anyone when he ordered Mosher to take out the top course of stones', noted Hoffmann.[24] Kaufmann eventually told Wright about the wall, saying that if Wright had not noticed it, it must not detract from the house. Wright calmly took Kaufmann under the terrace, showing him the cantilever that had held up under test loads for over a month without the new wall's support; the wall was removed. Throughout the construction, Wright exhibited total disdain for those who doubted the structural integrity of the house; after the first floor slab was set, but while it was still heavily braced with wooden framing, Wright made a show of walking under the house, even kicking out some of the wooden supports.

In the design and construction of Fallingwater, Wright displayed acute sensitivity to the natural site, attempting wherever possible to save trees and retain rock outcroppings in their original form. There was less excavation and removal of rock in the building of the house itself than that which occurred in the small quarry that served as the source for its rock walls. The concrete trellis over the drive curves dramatically in two places in order to go around the trunks of trees close to the walls of the house. The cantilevered floor slab of the west terrace, with its three transverse beams anchored directly into the huge boulder next to the driveway, had three holes in the basic structure framed around existing trees to save them and allow them to grow right through the slab when completed. Wright's suggestion that the concrete be given a finish coat of gold leaf was rejected by Kaufmann on the grounds that it did not belong in what he termed his informal 'mountain lodge', saving Wright from one of his less appropriate ideas. What Wright was after for the colour of the concrete was something that would appear to be of the earth, and the house today exhibits a harmonious blend of grey stone, light golden painted concrete, and 'Cherokee red' painted steel mullions.

In this attempt to create a place in harmony with nature, the windows at the kitchen and small bedrooms, without vertical framing at the stone wall, allow inside and outside to merge in a way very similar to the flagstones which are set in the floor so that the joints seem to continue beneath the glass doors out onto the terraces. While historians maintain that Kaufmann suggested running the glass directly into the stone, and some have even described (incorrectly) the stone slot as having been cut with a saw, the pattern of the rock wall, with the slot carefully left between the differing stone patterns on either side, leads us to suspect that Wright conceived this detail well before construction. Perhaps the most telling instance of Kaufmann's contributing to the 'natural' feeling of the house came in the living room with the original boulder that, emerging from the flat slate floor, served as the hearth for the house; Wright had intended to cut the boulder off flat, even with the slate floor, but – much to Wright's delight – Kaufmann suggested it remain as it was when his family used to picnic upon it before the house was built. Here we can see, even during construction, that Wright was ready to incorporate ideas that would enhance the spatial and experiential richness of his designs.

25

26

The experience of Fallingwater from without

The natural beauty of the extensive site is what we first notice upon arriving at Fallingwater.[25] As we walk through the woods, we are not aware of the house ahead, for Fallingwater does not dominate its site as country houses have traditionally done, by being placed on the top of the highest point or at the end of a cleared axis. Here we are introduced to the character and natural features of the landscape during our winding approach, noticing the rock walls, exposed by weather and stream erosion, composed of thin horizontal layers of Pottsville sandstone, varying from dark grey to a lighter buff colour. Near the stream grows the flowering rhododendron, and there are white, black and red oaks, birch, tulip, maple, hickory, butternut, apple and wild black cherry trees near the waterfall.[26] In the summer the house can hardly be seen due to the denseness of the green vegetation; in the autumn the coloured leaves, complementing the light golden colour of the concrete terraces, add an element of beauty that is extraordinary; in the winter, with snow cloaking the flat roofs and terraces, the house appears to be an extension of the flat rock layers of the waterfall more than at any other season. The rock walls at Fallingwater are directly related to the rock cliffs in Wright's home country,[27] the rock walls of Taliesin that he built from that inspiration, and finally the rock walls of the stream of Bear Run. Visitors who detect the close resemblance between the natural rock walls of the stream and the walls of Fallingwater are often surprised to discover the close relationship with Wright's works in the Wisconsin hills.

When the house first comes into view, we are somewhat surprised to see across the stream from us a series of horizontal terraces that float without visible means of support. We had expected our first view of the house to be the famous perspective from below the falls, Wright's favourite drawing of the design, and one that has been published so widely as to become the iconic image of Wright's work. While that famous view may be easily attained by turning left and descending the rock-cut stairs (put in by Wright) to reach the large level boulder in the middle of the stream below the falls, the more reserved perspective with which Wright introduces the house is worth considering. In his perceptive analysis, Robert Harrison has noted that Fallingwater's 'fame as a masterpiece of architectural design seems strangely at odds with the feature for which it is famous, namely its discretion ... the fact that the house not only comes to rest in its environment but also embodies an extension of the foundation upon which it rests'.[28] In this house, Wright has created a powerful dichotomy; the natural rock layers are repeated almost exactly, in thickness and random pattern of setting, in the vertical walls that emerge from the boulders above the waterfall, while the lighter-coloured horizontal reinforced concrete terraces and roof planes exfoliate from this rock wall core, cantilevering both along and across the stream. This opposition between vertical/mass/earth and horizontal/floating/sky reflects the natural condition found in the trees, their roots and trunks anchored to the earth and their limbs and leaves cantilevering out into thin air. The stability of the house, its rooted condition, is unexpectedly emphasized and reinforced by the flow of water under it; rather than undermining the anchored quality of the house, Harrison notes how 'the dynamic relation between flowing water and solid foundations'[29] imparts to the house a sense of repose on the earth – it appears to have grown from its site. Wright said that 'it is in the nature of any organic building to grow from its site, come out of the ground into the light – the ground itself held always as a component basic part of the building itself'.[30]

Standing across the stream, we are made more aware by the house of the forces underlying this typical forest clearing; in building this house, Wright transforms this space that could be anywhere in the forest into a specific place, a place that is remembered. Wright said: 'We start with the ground ... In any and every case the character of the site is the beginning of the building that aspires to architecture ... All must begin there where they stand'.[31] The house crystallizes and gives form to the vertical and horizontal tensions latent in the waterfall itself, exaggerating and thus making evident the vertical stacking of the rock layers in the natural cliff walls and the cantilever of the rock slabs over which the water cascades; as Wright said, 'In the stony bonework of the earth, the princi-

27

28

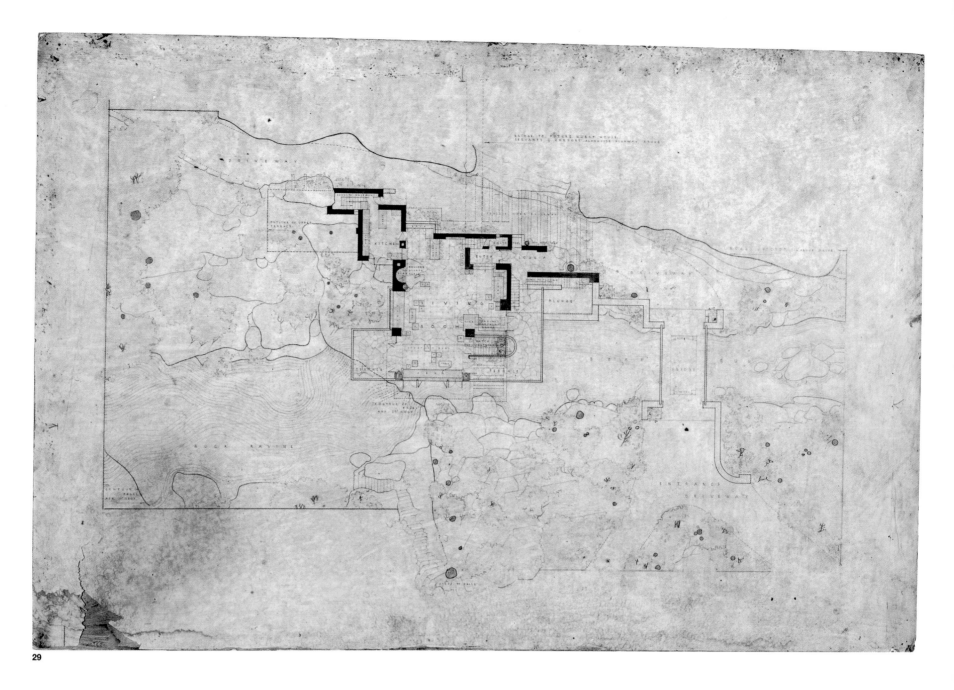

29

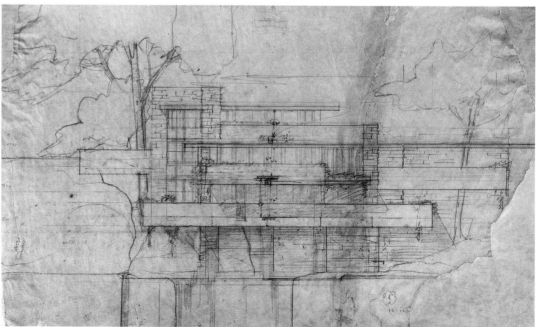

30

ples that shaped stone as it lies, or as it rises and remains to be sculpted by winds and tide – there sleep forms enough for all the ages, for all of man'.[32] What was a small and typical natural event along a stream becomes, with the construction of the house, a unique and habitable space where we are made far more aware of the waterfall and its natural surroundings than we could possibly have been before the house came to make this place. The house draws all the profiles of the landforms to itself, resolving them within its order; as Martin Heidegger said of a similar architectural and structural construction of landscape occupation and clarification, 'the bridge gathers the earth as landscape around the stream'.[33] The house-as-a-place brings the landscape into focus, into presence, to be experienced as part of human life. Only places where man has decided to dwell, can make the site fully present for us. Fallingwater does not stand on the site so much as it makes the site stand forth, 'building the site',[34] allowing it to come to our attention, to come into being as a human place, to become a place of memory.

The vertical rock walls make the house's actual anchorage to the ground, but the horizontal floating planes nevertheless still relate to the earth, in a larger sense. Wright said: 'I see this extended horizontal line as the true earth-line of human life, indicative of freedom. Always'.[35] Most important for Wright was the way in which the emphasis on the horizontal acted to ground the house, making it a true foundation for the life within; 'the horizontal planes in buildings, the planes parallel to the earth, identify themselves with the ground – make the building belong to the ground'.[36] In the forest, thick with trees and fractured by rock walls, Wright restates the horizontal as the datum of human dwelling, its freedom indicated by the way in which the horizontal concrete planes turn and interlock as they layer one above the other. As Harrison points out: 'the search for freedom in horizontality, and not in the celestial nostalgias of the vertical rise, makes of Wright an American in the exceptional, Thoreauvian sense. Whatever freedom we may call ours is to be found on the earth, whose surface is round only from a perspective beyond the earth. For those on the earth its surface extends horizontally, that is to say, constitutes a horizon. A house is that which gathers the horizon around itself'.[37] In Fallingwater, Wright creates shelter that is founded on the principle of this horizontal freedom and openness rather than the traditional understanding of closure. Yet the sense of shelter so evident even on the outside of Fallingwater comes from the fact that Wright built the house into its site, anchoring it to the earth, our only true shelter. The house provides shelter by opening to its site, rather than by closing itself off. Indeed, in rising from its foundations and opening onto its broad terraces, Fallingwater acts to unfold the sense of shelter latent in the earth itself – that which Wright called *unfolding* architecture as distinguished from *enfolding* architecture. Harrison states: 'if it is to provide this shelter, the earth must be drawn out of its closure by the house ... Wright reminds us that the earth tends to fold into itself, or to withdraw into its own closure, and that the earth cannot become a shelter unless it is unfolded, or disclosed, by human appropriation. It has become clear by now that [for Wright] appropriation does not mean acquisitive possession but the disclosure of freedom in the space of dwelling'.[38]

As we move around the house, our vantage point changes dramatically in height, from above the house to even with it to below it; the horizontal concrete planes and vertical rock walls constantly change position relative to one another, not allowing us to establish any static image of its exterior form. At the first floor, the main horizontal volume sits forward of the main vertical set of walls rising out of the back of the house and cantilevers in both directions parallel to the stream above the falls. The main horizontal volume of the second floor, which serves as the ceiling and roof of the floor below, nevertheless projects perpendicular to the stream bed. These two primary planes cross, one above the other, creating a composite cruciform and capturing the space of the living room at its centre. The third floor is set back, split by the vertical masonry mass, the horizontal planes stretching out to either side and again cantilevering parallel to the stream. As is typical in Wright's houses, we are more aware of the undersides than the tops of the horizontal planes; we sense how they cantilever

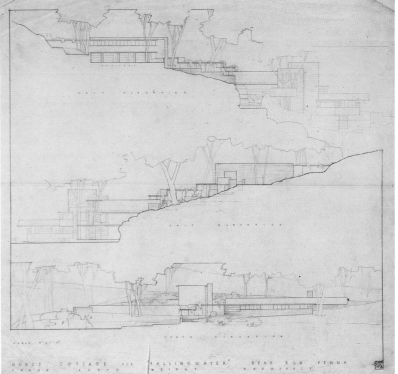

31

32 Final second and third floor plans, west and south elevations.
33 Construction drawings: sections, west and east elevations. As shown, the suspended stairs over the stream were not originally intended to have structural post bearing on stream bed.
34 Construction drawings: sections. As shown, boulder in lower right section C–C was originally intended to be cut off flat. At Kaufmann's suggestion, Wright left it in its existing condition, rounded and emerging from door to form the living room hearth.

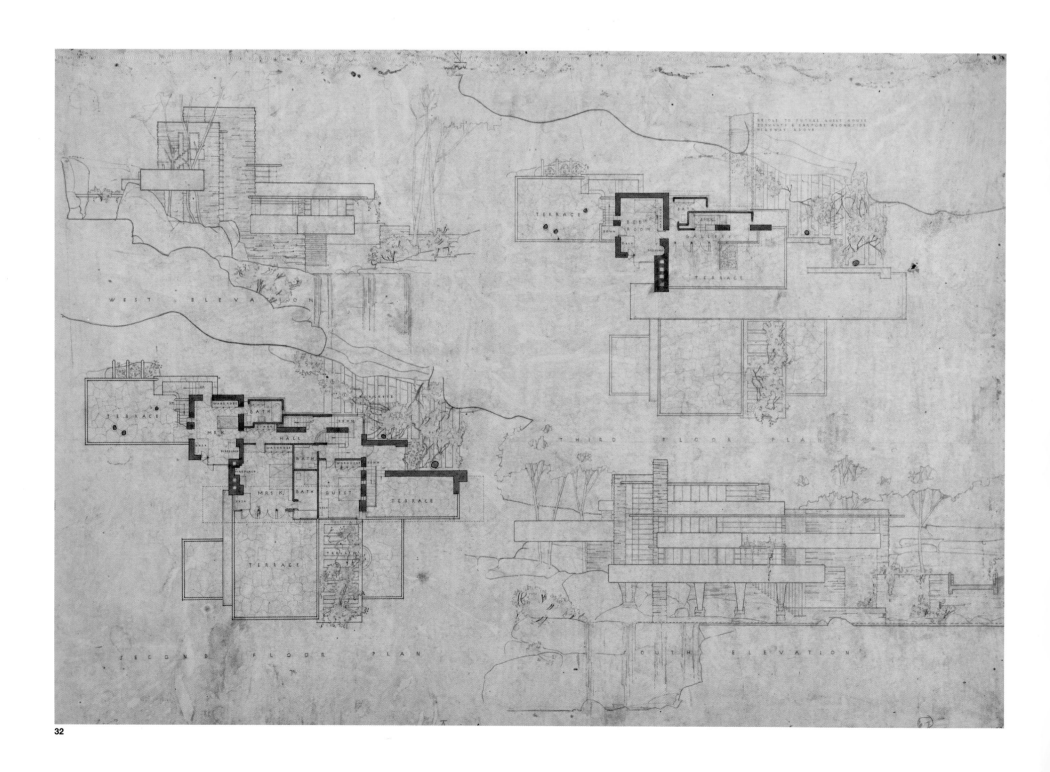

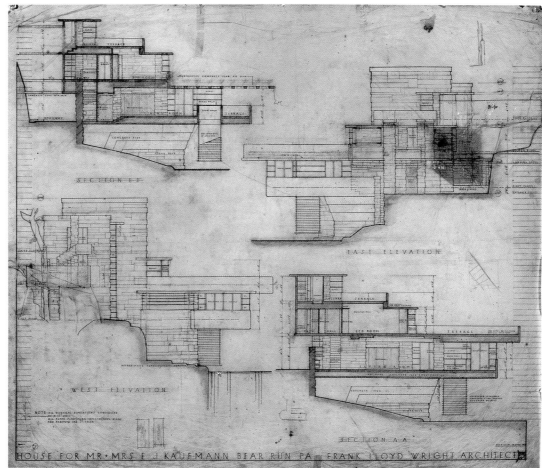

33

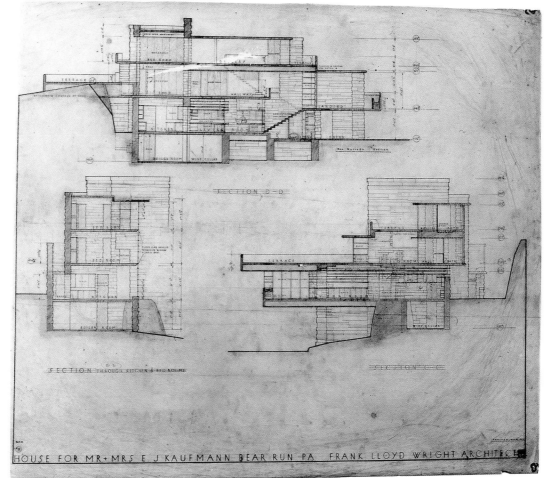

34

35

out to cover space, so that the upper portion of the stream above the falls feels as if it had been drawn into the volume of the house. The house is set against the north side of the stream, cut into a south-facing hillside, so that the sun plays across the three main elevations all day, producing strong shadows, sparkling off the water of the stream, and bringing out the colours of the house's materials. Looking more closely, we notice the glass, set back into the shadows, infilling between the horizontal concrete planes; the red-painted steel mullions only emerge into full view, running in a continuous rhythm up three storeys between the stone walls, when seen from below the waterfall.

In order to enter the house, we must turn away from the vantage point of the famous downstream perspective, walking up along the opposite side of the stream and crossing the bridge that Wright built to the right, or east, side of the house. Wright used an entry road that existed before the house was built as the driveway, which, after crossing this bridge, wraps around and disappears to the left behind the house. The bridge consists of a U-shaped reinforced concrete element, with four square lights set under glass at the corners of the slab, spanning between parallel rock walls on either side of the stream. The view of the house from the bridge is arresting; the darker vertical rock walls are layered one behind the other, stepping up the side of the hill to the right, while the lighter horizontal reinforced concrete slabs and terraces project far out to the left over the stream. The simple span of the bridge on which we stand, supported at both ends, makes us all the more aware of the extent to which the house cantilevers out from its foundations, supported only at one end. The stream is quite shallow here as it moves across the flat face of the bedrock ledge upon which the house sits, and a set of stairs, suspended from the concrete slab above, descend from the living room to a small landing just above the surface of the water. On the right side of the stream, a low wall contains a deep plunge pool carved into the rock, with steps down to it hidden behind the taller rock wall supporting the terrace above. Where Wright has positioned us on the bridge, we can hear the waterfall but not see it as the stream disappears over the edge of the rock ledge at the other end of the house. In order to enter the house and overlook the waterfall from the cantilevered terrace, we cannot approach it directly, as we must move across the bridge. Through its glass wall at our eye-level, we can see directly into and through the living room, floating out over the stream, but as in almost all of Wright's houses, we cannot enter the main room directly, but must move along the edges of the house, around its perimeter, searching for the entrance which is always hidden from the initial view. Utilizing the fact that in architecture the path of the eye can be quite different from the path of the body, Wright lets us catch glimpses of our destination, inviting us to enter the house and rediscover from within what we have first seen or heard from without.

The experience of Fallingwater from within
We cross the bridge and turn left, seeing that the driveway, cut into the natural rock wall of the hill behind before Fallingwater was built, runs between the hillside and the stepped series of rock walls at the back of the house. A trellis of

reinforced concrete spans from the rock walls of the house to the rock wall of the hillside, its beams curved occasionally to allow trees existing on the site before the house was built to pass through it undisturbed. To the left an opening between the layered rock walls lets us into a loggia: to the left is a view through suspended concrete stairs to the living room terrace; to the right a small fountain shoots a thin stream of water into a basin set into the earth. Ahead is the front door, made like the windows of glass set in red steel frames, deeply recessed between rock walls, a concrete slab header forming a low ceiling over the entry, the glass above coming forward. As Hoffmann notes, 'Wright's feeling for the site was so keen that the act of crossing the bridge (a span of 28 feet) and approaching the entrance of the house (60 feet past the bridge) would always seem an uphill journey into a private territory, even though the entrance (at three steps below the living room floor) was at an elevation only six inches higher than the bridge roadway'.[39]

Opening the door we move into a small foyer, rock walls directly ahead and to our right; we turn to the opening at the left, towards the living room. Before mounting the three stairs up to the living room floor, we should notice that from the level of this lower foyer, our eye-level is almost exactly at the centre of the space between floor and ceiling. From this brief vantage point, the two horizontal planes are perfectly balanced, the smooth white plaster ceiling above and the rippling dark flagstone floor below, seeming to completely define the space, with only the thin steel mullions of the windows and two square stone piers standing between them – no walls can be seen save those that enclose us at the entry. From this perspective, the living room seems to open out in all directions, so that upon passing through the small cave-like entry we find, much to our surprise, that we can look out to the trees on on all sides. Rising only slightly at the room's centre to house recessed lighting, Hoffmann points out how 'the lower ceiling plane near the brighter walls of glass at the perimeter would give a certain velocity to the outward flow of space, toward broad horizontal vistas'.[40] Moving up the three steps, we are struck by the difference our higher viewpoint makes in our perception of the living room; the ceiling (only seven feet one inch in height) is now very close to our heads and the flagstone floor now dominates our view. With the light coming towards us from the windows all around, the reflections off the flagstone floor make it appear strikingly similar to the water of the stream below.

Upon entering the living room, we are surrounded by low walls with built-in bookcases, desks and long seats, the only exception being the glass doors diagonally across the room. Drawn towards the sound of the waterfall, we walk across the living room and open these glass doors, moving out onto the terrace cantilevered out over the waterfall. Looking out into the trees, the sound of the waterfall now surrounds us and we seem now to be a part of it, having been projected out into space directly above. At this moment we recognize Wright's intention in placing the house where he did; rather than present the waterfall as an object to be looked at, he allows us to feel as if we are part of it, hearing it and sensing it, but rarely seeing it from within the house. The American philosopher

35 Living room. Diagonal view towards fireplace and dining table, as seen from top of 'hatch' or suspended stairs.

36 Construction drawings: glass hatch over suspended stairs at living room; plan, elevation and section.

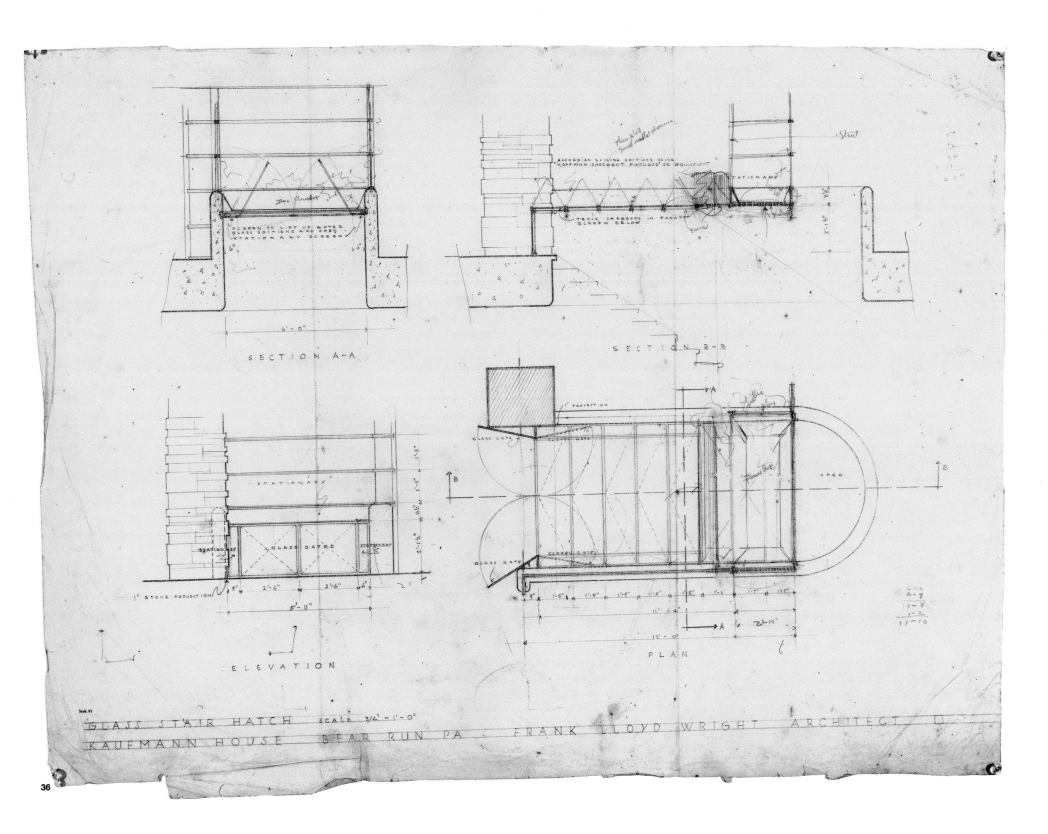

John Dewey has noted that 'the eye is the sense of distance', while 'sound itself is near, intimate;'[41] Wright himself actively engages this difference in our experience of Fallingwater. In this way, the waterfall never becomes merely an image for the house's inhabitants, as it does in the famous perspectival view from below, but remains something that underlies our entire experience, permeating all of our senses, including most strongly our hearing and our haptic sense – the sense of bodily position and movement in space.

This feeling of being suspended over the waterfall is reinforced and confirmed as we are drawn back into the room towards the bright light coming from the trellis and skylights opened in the concrete roof directly ahead; a low glass-enclosed 'hatch' opens to the concrete stair that we saw earlier descending to the stream below. The dark grey colour of the bedrock ledge under the shallow water, and the way light is reflected from the rippling surface of the stream, are matched exactly by the grey flagstone floor upon which we stand. Seen through the hatch, the suspended stairs oppose the flow of the water in the stream, and the movement down to the water is balanced by the skylight and trellis openings to the sky above. Descending to the stream below, we enter the large exterior space covered by the main concrete floor slab of the house, only ten feet above the surface of the stream. Behind us to our left, seen through the open risers of the stair, are the three piers angled out to support the house above, the dark space underneath the house open all the way back to the boulders of the hillside. Ahead is the bridge, to the left the rock walls, plunge pool and sculpture, to the right the natural stream bank; we are hovering only inches above the water, facing away from the waterfall, roaring behind us.

Ascending the stairs and emerging again into the living room, we turn to the right; diagonally across the room is the fireplace: large, heavy, its fire flickering from the darkness of the rock walls anchoring the back of the house. This fireplace is not set into the wall – it *is* the wall, a half-cylinder cavity running from floor to plaster soffit, the hearth the boulder of the site itself, emerging from the floor; Hoffmann notes: 'Indoors the [flagstones of the floor] were sealed and waxed, but the boulder was not. It came through the floor like the dry top of a boulder peering above the stream waters'.[42] A red spherical kettle is set into a hemispherical niche in the stone to one side, suspended on a steel pivot that allows it to be swung over the fire. The buffet is built in along the back wall under a high window to the right of the fireplace, and the built-in dining table, centred exactly on the main volume of the living room that projects out across the stream, similarly projects from the back wall into the room itself. We are now aware that within the rectangular volume of this room, centred by the two stone piers that make a square with the entry wall and fireplace, there is a counter-pointing pair of strong diagonal axes: that between the stair down to the stream and the fireplace, both vertically-oriented (water-sky and rock-sky) and opening on the edge of the primary volume of the living room; and that between the entry and the terrace over the waterfall, both horizontally-oriented and contained in volumes projected off the corners of the primary volume of the living room (together creating a pinwheel with the living room). These two axes between four

pivotal 'places' within the house give the cruciform geometric volumes of the whole a diagonal pattern of use or inhabitation, reinforced by the fact that, as is typical in Wright's houses, the doors into the room open at its corners.

In the corner between the fireplace and dining table is the door to the kitchen, which is enclosed on almost all sides by the stone walls anchoring the house to its site. The light in the kitchen comes from the stacked horizontal windows that turn a corner, leaving space for a narrow casement. The view out from this cave-like kitchen to the terrace floating over the waterfall, set at the same floor level, gives the most succinct experience of the oppositions Wright built into and balanced in this house. This is again encountered in the stairs which climb up between stone walls to the second floor, beginning across from the kitchen door, behind the entry foyer. What we might normally expect to find – the heavier falling towards the ground and the lighter rising towards the sky – is reversed when we notice that the solid, heavy, stone stairs go *up*, while the open, light, concrete stairs at the hatch go *down*. That this is not coincidental becomes evident when we see that the points where the two stairs start their respective ascent and descent from the flagstone floor are aligned along the same edge of the living room, suggesting that Wright intended us to perceive the stairs as the two sides of a single experience of gravitational reversal made possible by the cantilevered, hillside section of the house, grounded by the flagstone floor of the living room. Our penetration down through the stone floor to find light stairs floating over water which reflects the sky overhead, combined with our penetration up through layers of solid stone to finally emerge, unexpectedly, at the tree-tops rather than at their roots, make this one of the most astonishing and richly suggestive movement sequences in all of Wright's work.

The second floor hall leads to the master bedroom, the fireplace of which exhibits the most dynamic stonework in the entire house. The large rectangular stones of the mantel and adjacent shelves cantilever asymmetrically towards the hearth in a manner similar to the way the house as a whole projects out over the stream. Through glass doors opens a terrace far larger than the bedroom itself; the scale of this terrace demands that it be understood as the second 'great room' of the house – an outdoor room above the living room, with unencumbered views out in three directions. From this vantage point, we can see that the flagstone floors of the house and terraces, so similar to the water's surface, repeat at higher and higher levels the layered planes begun by the two horizontal surfaces of the stream, below and above the falls – just as the rock walls extend the rock layers of the stream bed outcroppings. The large volume of the terrace is complemented by the subtlety of Wright's use of wood graining along the opposite wall; the door into the master bedroom has the wood grain running vertically from floor to ceiling, while the built-in cupboards and cabinets, cantilevered off the wall with four inches left open at top and bottom, have the wood grain running horizontally. This reminds us of the similar ordering of the window mullions in the house; the operable doors and windows have vertical proportions while the fixed windows have horizontal proportions, often with butt-glazing at the corners to eliminate the vertical member altogether.

37 Preliminary west elevation of living room, looking towards fireplace and kitchen door.

38 Preliminary construction drawing: suspended stairs below glass hatch at living room; plan, elevation and structural details. Note addition of structural post bearing on stream bed.

39 Preliminary design drawing for living room fireplace. Plan and elevation with swinging kettle shown in both 'in' and 'out' positions.

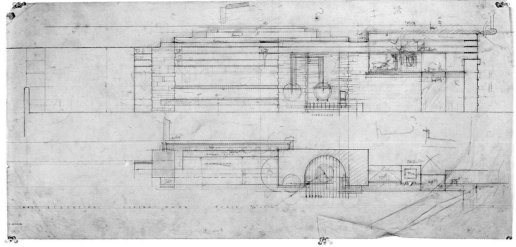

37

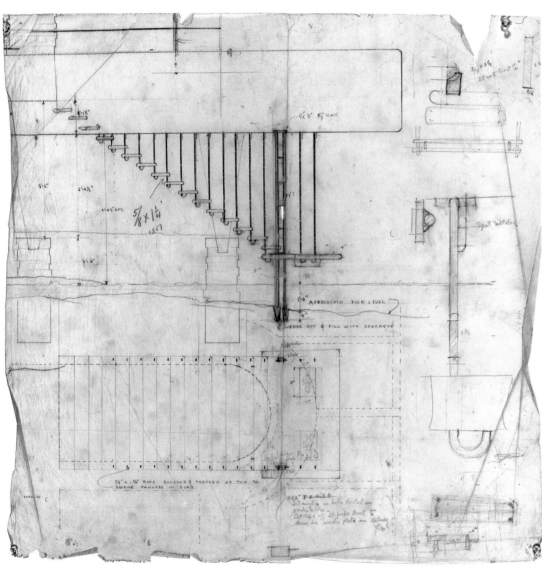

38

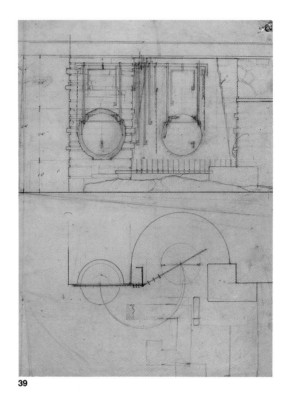

39

The bedroom used by Mr Kaufmann is over the kitchen, with the same sense of cave-like, rock-walled refuge. Up a few stairs at the back a long terrace cantilevers to the west of the house, anchoring to a freestanding boulder with a series of concrete ribs. The stair to the third floor has wooden bookshelves set into the horizontal joints of the stonework, similar to shelves appearing above the fireplace and dining table in the living room. On the third floor is a long gallery facing a smaller terrace, and the bedroom used by Edgar Kaufmann, Jr, sits above that used by his father, with which its shares the west terrace. In both of these small bedrooms and in the kitchen, the stonework of the fireplace wall seems to pass right through the glass from inside to outside, due to Wright's careful provision of a vertical slot between the stones that allows the glass to be set directly into the stone, without any kind of frame; there is no more telling detail in Fallingwater, and Wright's intention 'to bring the outside world into the house and let the inside of the house go outside'[43] is here given its perfect interpretation. In these rooms he also achieves the perfect open corner, for the corner is made by two small casement windows which, when opened, cause the corner to disappear altogether. In these small rooms, the irregular horizontal layers of the stone walls are integrated with the regular horizontal rhythm of the steel window mullions and the shifting wooden planes of the built-in bookshelves and tabletops to produce a true sense of shelter, combining the attributes of refuge and outlook.[44]

Fallingwater appears to us to have grown out of the ground and into the light, making present the latent power of the boulder on which it sits above the waterfall – the same boulder which emerges from the rippling 'water' of the flagstone living room floor to provide a place of stability in front of the fireplace. The natural setting is so integrated into this house that in occupying it we are constantly reminded of where we are by the sound of the waterfall, the flow of space and movement inside and outside across the floors and terraces, the fire burning in the bedrock masonry of the house giving a sense of refuge, while the views and sunlight are framed by the steel windows, which act as spatial 'nets' or 'webs' similar to the weaving of stained glass in Wright's earlier houses. The whole is carefully calibrated to the scale and eye-level of the inhabitant; the degree to which Wright formed his designs to respond to human comfort and the rituals of daily life is rarely acknowledged, despite his statement that 'human use and comfort should not be taxed to pay dividends on any designer's idiosyncrasy. Human use and comfort should have intimate possession of every interior – should be felt in every exterior'.[45] Particularly in the living room, the primary room of the house containing entry, library, living and dining, Fallingwater appears to us as a place that calls for inhabitation; it seems empty and meaningless without the human figure occupying its spaces, acting out the rituals of daily life. In what sounds remarkably like a description of Fallingwater, Dewey described an ideal relation between architecture, dwelling and landscape by saying: 'Through going out into the environment, position unfolds into volume; through the pressure of environment, mass is retracted into energy of position, and space remains, when matter is contracted, as an opportunity for further action'.[46]

The rediscovery of fundamental dwelling

Lillian Kaufmann once sent Wright a birthday card in which she wrote: 'Living in a house built by you has been my one education'.[47] In Fallingwater Wright captured the perfect essence of our desire to live with nature, to dwell in a forested place and be at home in the natural world. Edgar Kaufmann, Jr, on the day he donated Fallingwater to the public after living in it for 25 years, said: 'Its beauty remains fresh like that of the nature into which it fits. It has served well as a house, yet has always been more that that: a work of art, beyond any ordinary measures of excellence ... House and site together form the very image of man's desire to be at one with nature, equal and wedded to nature ... Such a place cannot be possessed'.[48] To visit Fallingwater, as to live in it, is an education in the potential of architectural design. We cannot help feeling that the house is intended as the setting for communing with nature: the stairs down to the stream; the boulder-hearth emerging from the flagstone floor; and the all-permeating sound of the waterfall confirm this initial impression. We are not the same after occupying it as we were when we entered; our perceptions have been both broadened and deepened, our experience has been profoundly moving; yet we are aware, Hoffmann notes, that Fallingwater 'reveals itself slowly, and never once and for all'.[49]

Fallingwater opened a new chapter in American architecture, and is perhaps rightly considered Wright's greatest work, for he was first and foremost an architect of houses. In its careful yet startling integration of ancient stone walls anchored to the bedrock and modern reinforced concrete terraces hovering in space, Connors states that Fallingwater may be understood as 'one of the great critiques of the modern movement in architecture, and simultaneously one of its masterpieces'.[50] Yet we cannot help feeling that there is more to this design than even that; this is an architecture that seizes our imagination, letting us see space and inhabitation in ways that seem new, but which we simultaneously feel to be ancient, somehow fundamental to our human nature. Gaston Bachelard said that 'discoveries made about the structure of space and time always react on the structure of the mind',[51] yet Fallingwater, and indeed all of Wright's work, would perhaps better be thought of as a rediscovery of the possibilities of dwelling in space and time. In this Wright was perhaps one of the only architects of our time to engage fundamental ancient principles in the creation of interior space, seeking the space within which was defined without boundaries; defined instead by the rituals of daily experience. Fallingwater is such a place, hovering among the leaves of the trees yet anchored to the bedrock of the earth, its spaces in flowing motion yet the whole a stable mass read against the movement of the stream; our experience of it that of a cave-like refuge yet also that of a free-floating outlook. As Wright said in 1936: 'An idea (probably rooted deep in instinct) that *shelter* should be the essential look of any dwelling. I came to see a building primarily not as a cave but as a broad shelter in the open, related to vista; vista without and vista within. You may see in these various feelings all taking the same direction that I was born an American, child of the ground and of space'.[52]

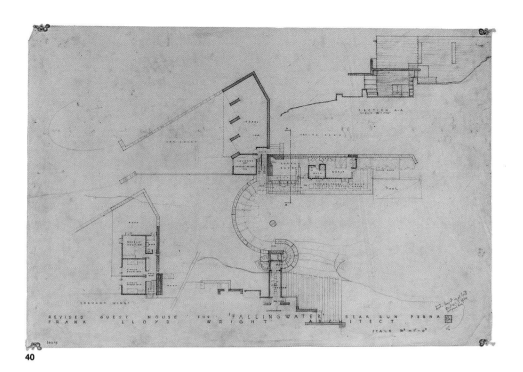

40 Fallingwater guest house
and garage. Final plans and
section.

41 Bridge over drive and
covered walkway from main
house to guest house. Plan,
elevation and sketch perspective
as seen from above.

40

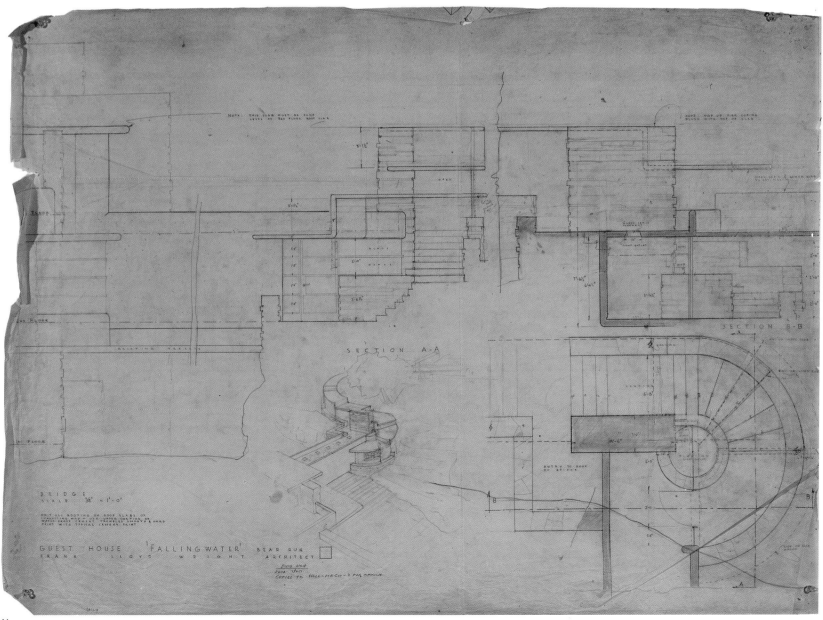

41

Left and centre Fallingwater
from without. Horizontal planes
projecting from a stone core,
cantilevered out over the waterfall, allowing the occupants to
inhabit a series of layered spaces
starting with the surface of the
stream below, continuing with
the flagstone-covered terraces
floating one above the other,
and terminating in the foliage
of the trees.

Right The house seen through
the trees from the hillside on the
opposite bank of the stream.
Similar to the view first seen in
approaching the house, we are
looking directly into the elevation, which from this vantage
point appears to be composed
of a series of floating horizontal
planes with no apparent means
of support. While the forms of
the house seem suggestive of
motion, the house as a whole is
paradoxically read as stable
against the constant actual
motion of the stream that
flows beneath it.

Fallingwater takes on differing readings with the changing seasons; spring, summer, autumn and winter each bring out specific aspects of the design, from the emphasis on the horizontal stacked stone and terraces when they are covered with snow, to the golden colour of the concrete and red of the steel window mullions which echo the leaves in autumn.

Left Views of the covered walkway leading from the main house to the guest house, an astonishingly agile, asymmetrical, folded, reinforced concrete structure that leads in a spiral up the hill to the guest house above.
Right The terrace on the guest house looks out to the south over the main house, and is covered by a low roof, with trellis-like openings, which terminates the folded roof over the walkway.

From the entry bridge, the solid vertical stone wall anchors the house to the right as the concrete planes project out over the stream to the left. While its sound is powerfully present, the waterfall cannot be seen from this vantage point, and we must enter the house to experience both the stream, on the stairs suspended just above its surface, and the waterfall itself, which can only be seen looking over the terrace on the other side of the living room from where we stand – thus we are invited to enter the house.

The composition of powerful anchorage and support, palpably present in the beams buried in the rock outcropping behind the upper bedroom terrace, and spaces suspended without any visible means of support, as in the terrace floating out over the waterfall (here seen from above), exemplifies the extraordinary capacity of this house to condense and make present the experiential possibilities of architectural construction.

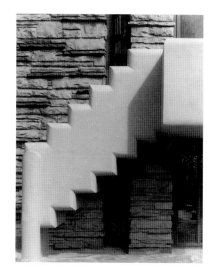

Left The hearth of the living room fireplace is the top of the bedrock boulder which rises right through the flagstone floor like a dry rock breaking through the surface of the stream. The boulder originally remained unwaxed, so that it literally appeared dry next to the waxed and reflective flagstones. The spherical kettle swings out of its hemispherical niche in the stone fireplace wall and hangs over the fire, allowing drinks to be heated.

Centre Diagonally across the living room from the fireplace is the glass 'hatch' covering the stairs suspended over the surface of the stream. From this vantage point we become aware that the surface of the stream and the waxed flagstones of the floor upon which we stand are exactly the same colour and texture.

Right The oppositions between anchorage and projection are powerfully summarized in the view from the kitchen, where we stand within a cave-like room made of rock and look towards the terrace suspended out into space over the waterfall.

The living room is defined by the shimmering, water-like flagstone floors and the smooth, precise, light ceiling floating overhead – each of these surfaces, while constructed of heavy materials, seems transformed by the space and light flowing and floating under and over us. Sunlight and exterior views enter all around as the walls are largely dissolved into glass curtains, allowing us to be suspended over stream or waterfall, while simultaneously being housed within this refuge anchored into the earth.

Left The second floor bedroom of Edgar Kaufmann has a built-in wood desk with a quarter circle cut out to allow the casement window to open, and bookshelves are let into the joints in the stone.

Centre and far right The master bedroom, used by Lillian Kaufmann, has a built-in closet with the wood grains ordered to complement the vertical and horizontal patterns of the window mullions of the house, and a fireplace that interlocks with the built-in desk, exhibiting the most dynamic stonework in the entire house. The stone stairs leading to the third floor are flanked by wooden bookshelves that are spaced on the pattern of the stair treads.

Right The guest house contains a single expansive room, the bedroom screened by the bathroom block, the entry demarcated from the living room by a simple wall of open wood slats, and the whole lined to the north by a narrow band of high clerestory windows, providing cooling cross-ventilation.

Left In Edgar Kaufmann's bedroom (and in the study above), the glass of the windows is set directly into the stone wall, without framing at the edge. This detail, perhaps more than any other, summarizes Wright's intentions for this house through the way in which it brings the outside in and the inside out, and in the manner in which it juxtaposes opposite formal, structural, material and experiential aspects of architecture – in this case the delicate, light, ephemeral glass pushing into the rough, heavy, rustic stone wall.

Below The third floor gallery – later made his bedroom by Edgar Kaufmann, Jr – compresses this experience of opposites, bringing into close proximity the horizontal extension and release from gravity, found on the terraces cantilevered out into the treetops, and the vertical anchorage and celebration of gravity, found in the stacked bedrock slabs that comprise the room's rear walls. In all these experiences, this house, a paradoxical space of resolved oppositions, finally reveals itself as a primal homage to the site and a place for ritual communion with nature.

Site plan
1 main home
2 guest house and garage
3 entry drive

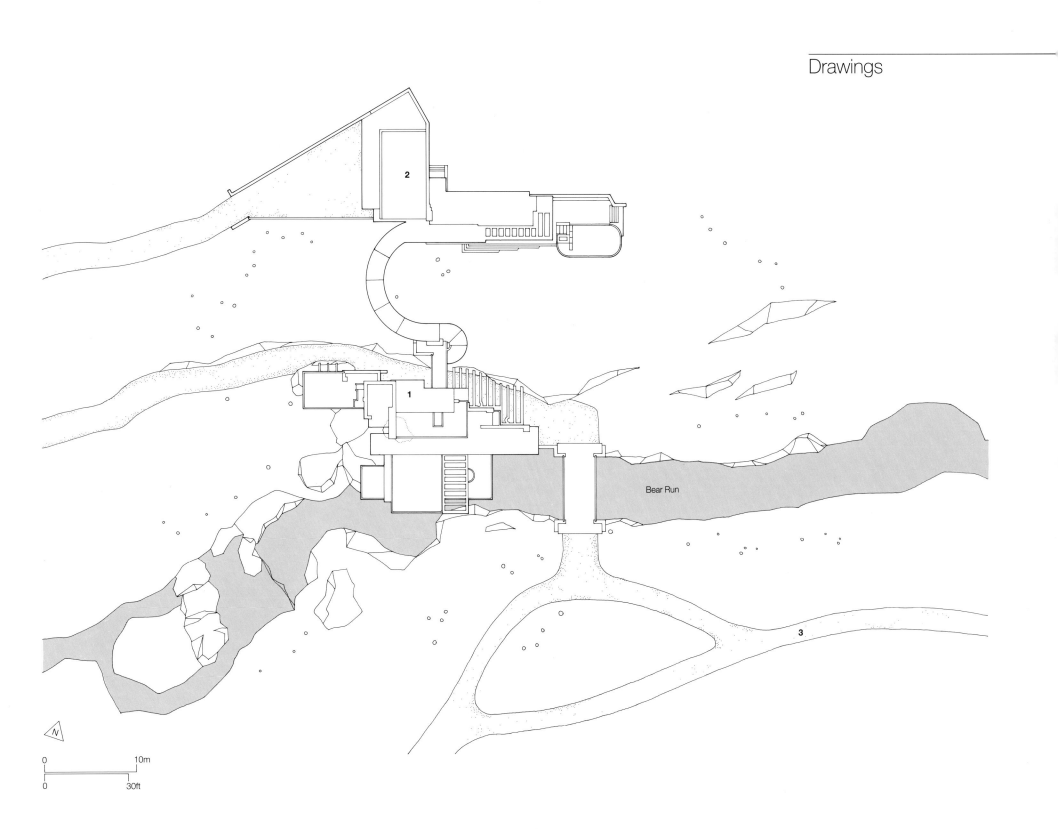

Bear Run

Floor plans

1 entry loggia
2 dining room
3 living room
4 kitchen
5 servants' quarters
6 waterfall terrace
7 east living room terrace
8 plunge pool
9 hatch – stairway to stream
10 bridge
11 master bedroom
12 master bedroom terrace
13 guest bedroom
14 west bedroom
15 west bedroom terrace
16 bridge across drive
17 study
18 gallery
19 gallery terrace

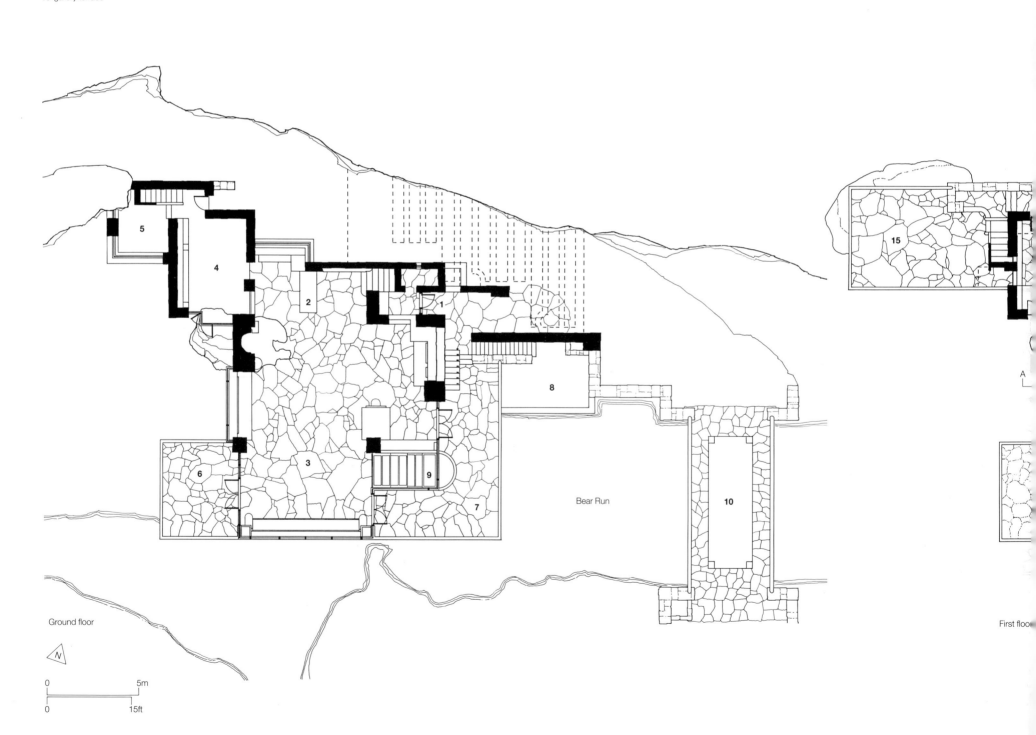

Ground floor

First floor

Bear Run

N

0   5m

0   15ft

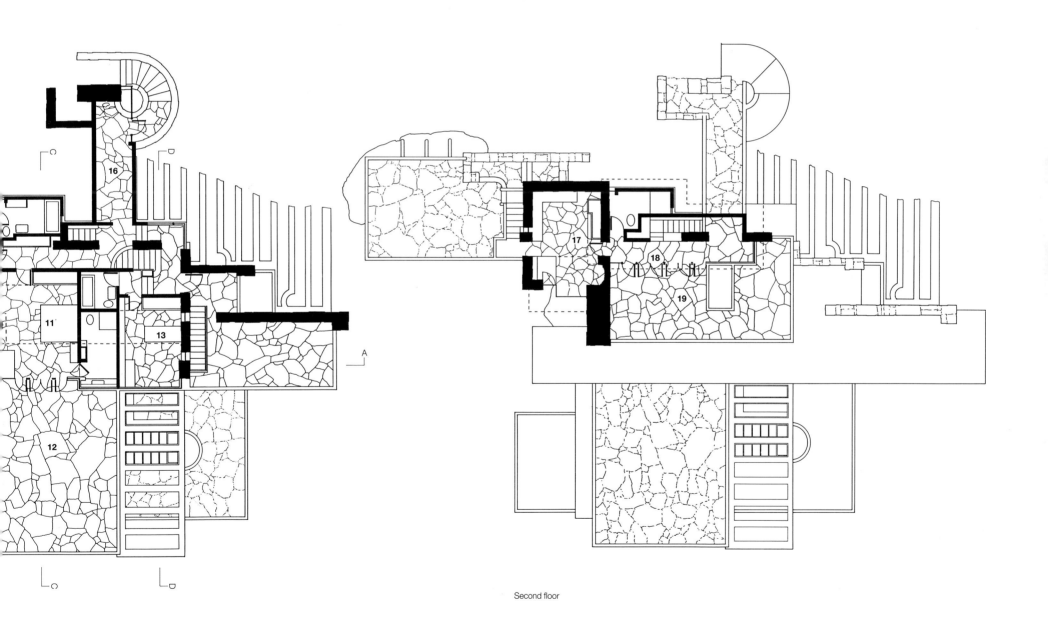

Second floor

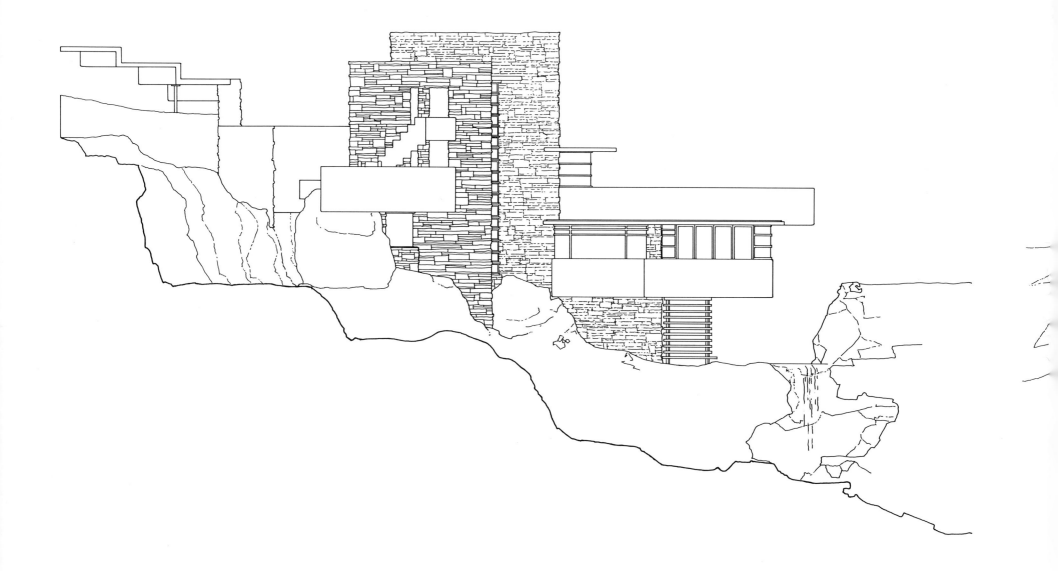

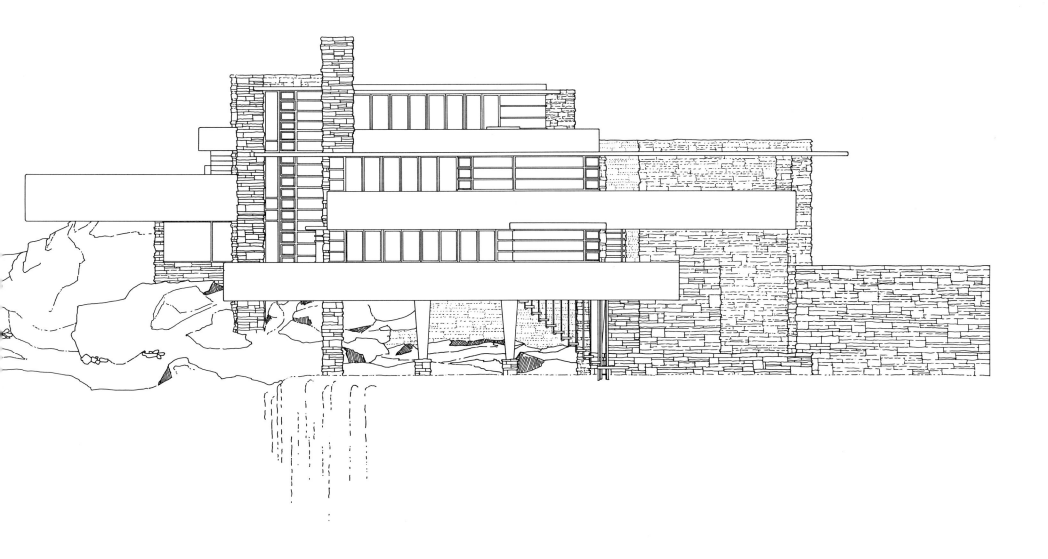

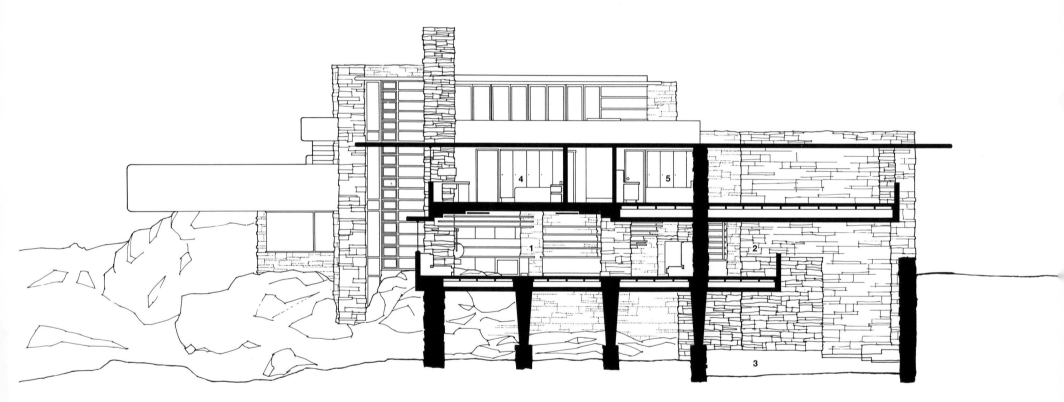

Section AA looking north

0   3m

0   10ft

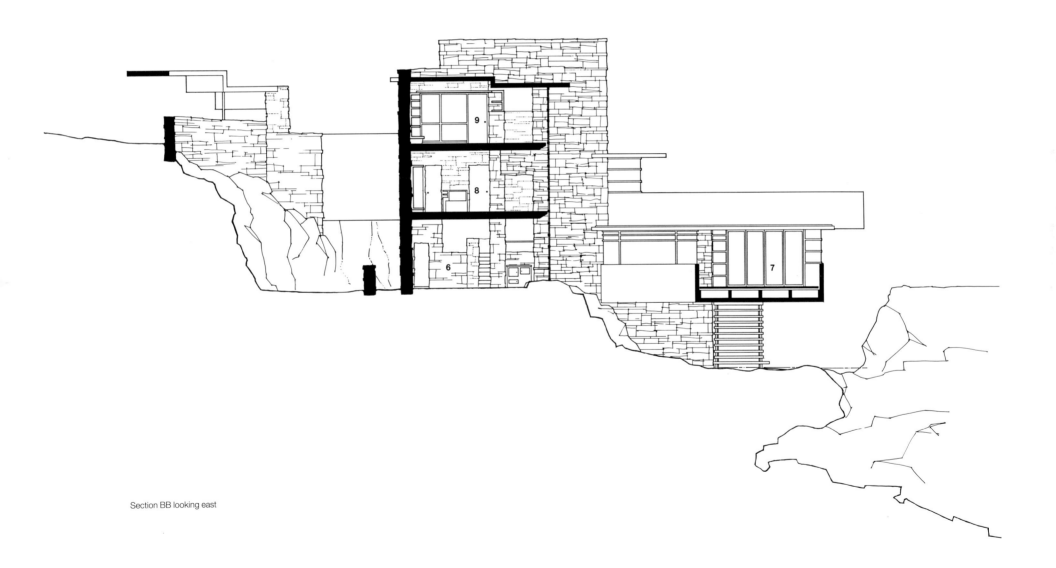

Section BB looking east

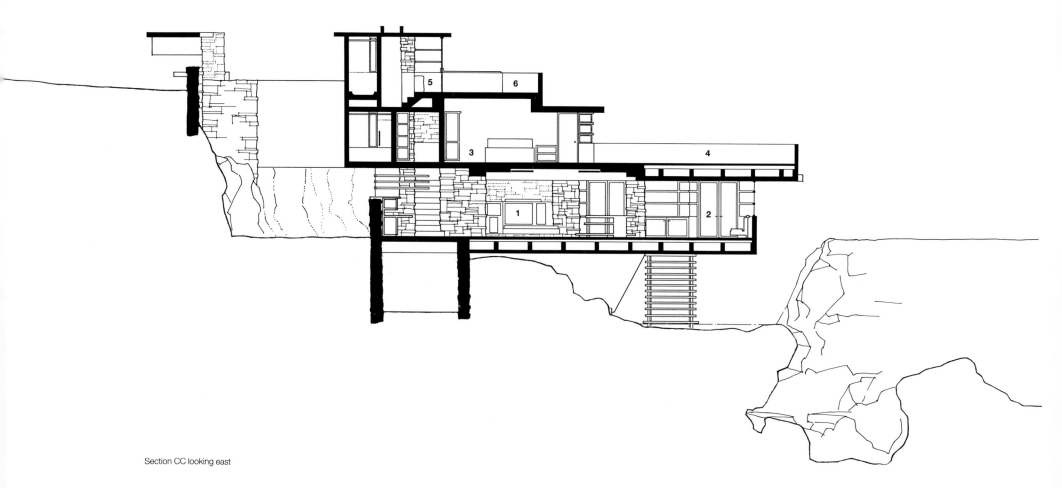

Section CC looking east

0   3m

0   10ft

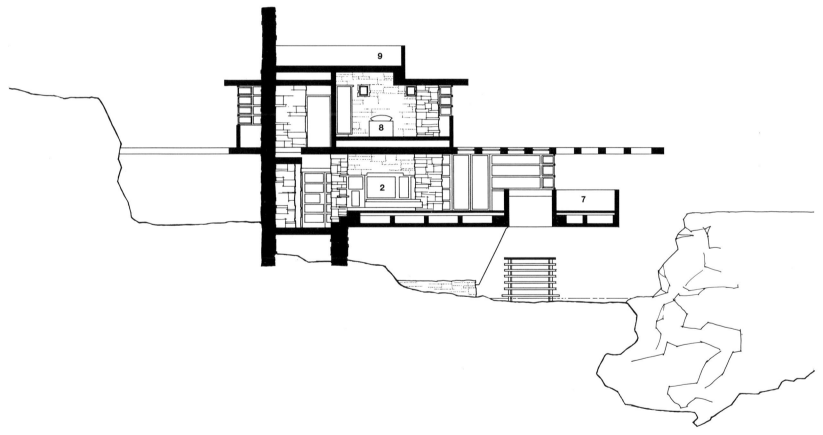

Section DD looking east

Living room

1 bookshelves
2 table
3 cupboard
4 seat
5 stairs
6 lamp standard
7 radiator
8 hatch

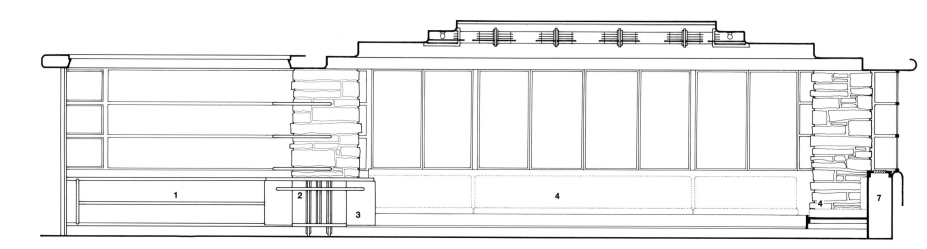

South elevation

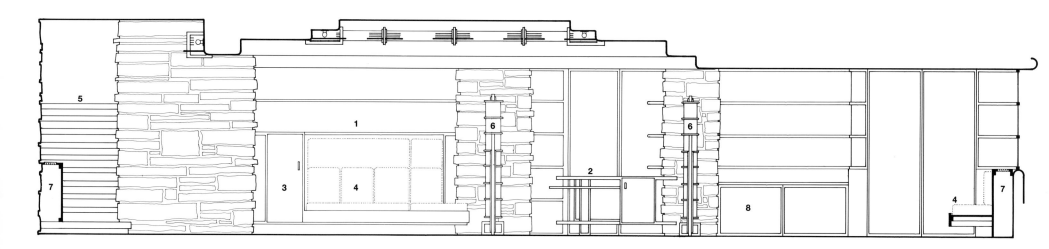

East elevation

Living room hearth with wine kettle

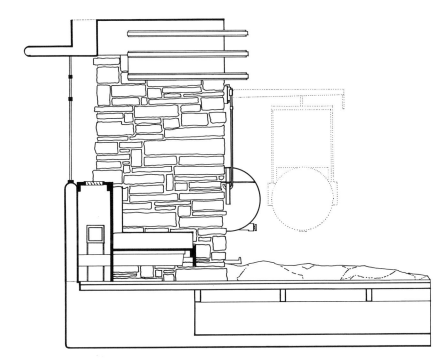

Section

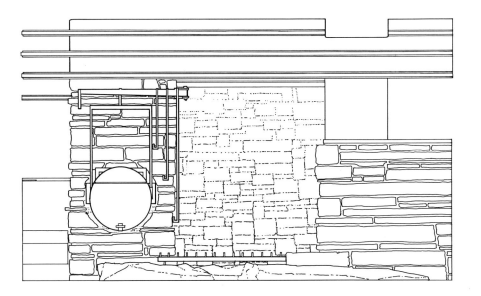

Elevation

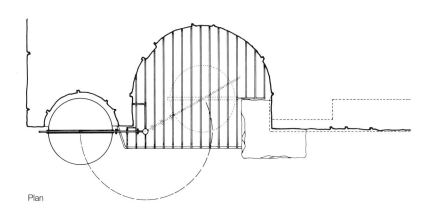

Plan

0   1m

0   3ft

Author's acknowledgements

I would like to thank the following people, whose efforts were essential to the completion of this book: The new drawings prepared for this publication were made by Robert Blatter and James Buzbee, who, along with fourteen other undergraduate and graduate students in the University of Florida's Department of Architecture, participated in a seminar I taught on Wright's drawings during the summer of 1993. Cathy Duncan, another participant in that seminar, researched and secured reproduction rights for photographic and drawing material used in this publication. Edward Teague, Librarian for the University of Florida Fine Arts and Architecture Library, provided information used in assembling the bibliography. Of the sources of illustrations, I would in particular like to thank Oscar Munoz, of the Frank Lloyd Wright Archives, who provided reproductions of Wright's drawings, and Janet Parks and Angela Giral of the Avery Architectural Library at Columbia University, who made available important photographic material. The published research of Donald Hoffmann and recollections of Edgar Kaufmann, Jr, are essential reading for anyone wishing to understand in depth the history of Fallingwater, and I have drawn upon them regularly in this text. I must thank my fellow faculty members and my students, who have endured a sometimes distracted department chair and teacher during the period I was writing this and other texts on Wright, and I owe many thanks to Dean Wayne Drummond, who has supported my perhaps atypical activity. Finally, thanks to James Steele, on whose recommendation I became involved in this project.

Illustration sources

(Numbers quoted refer to figure numbers, unless otherwise stated.) Avery Architectural and Fine Arts Library and Archives, Columbia University, New York: 11, 25, 26, 27, 28; Carnegie Institute Museum of Art, Chicago Historical Society (photograph Hedrich Blessing): 7; Fallingwater/Western Pennsylvania Conservancy: 9, 10, and colour photographs p 31 (photographs by Robert P Ruschak and Thomas A Heinz); Donald Hoffmann: 5; Frank Lloyd Wright Archives, copyright Frank Lloyd Wright Foundation, 1993: 1, 2, 3, 4, 12, 13, 14, 15, 16, 17, 18, 19, 20, 21, 22, 23, 24, 29, 30, 31, 32, 33, 34, 36, 37, 38, 39, 40, 41.

Notes

1 George Steiner, *Tolstoy or Dostoevsky*, New York: Vintage/Random House, 1959, p 3.

2 Joseph Connors, *The Robie House of Frank Lloyd Wright*, Chicago: University of Chicago Press, 1984, p 63.

3 Brendan Gill, *Many Masks: A Life of Frank Lloyd Wright*, New York: Putnam's, 1987, p 326.

4 Edgar Kaufmann, Jr, *Fallingwater: A Frank Lloyd Wright Country House*, New York: Abbeville Press, 1986, p 36. The younger Kaufmann, never having intended to be an architect, went on to become an important art historian, and one of Wright's chief interpreters. This beautifully-illustrated book gives his own recollections of the history of the house with which he was so closely associated.

5 Donald Hoffmann, *Frank Lloyd Wright's Fallingwater, The House and Its History*, New York: Dover, 1978, pp 8–10. Most of the factual information on the site, design and construction of Fallingwater used herein is drawn from this book, which is the definitive historical study of this house. Hoffmann's exhaustive investigation of the history of Fallingwater is essential reading for those desiring the full story of this extraordinary building.

6 Frank Lloyd Wright, *In the Cause of Architecture* (1928), F Gutheim, ed, reprint of *Architectural Record* essays, New York: McGraw-Hill, 1975, p 153.

7 For the various versions, see Hoffmann, op cit, pp 15–17. For Mosher and Tafel's version, as well as Tafel's memories of the construction, see Edgar Tafel, *Apprentice to Genius: Years with Frank Lloyd Wright* (1979), reprint, New York: Dover, 1985, pp 1–9.

8 Hoffmann, op cit, p 17.

9 Blaine Drake, an apprentice, recalls this in a letter quoted in Hoffmann, op cit, p 15.

10 Bob Mosher, in a 1974 letter quoted in Hoffmann, op cit, p 17.

11 Wright, in an interview with Hugh Downs, 1953, Frank Lloyd Wright, *The Future of Architecture*, New York: Horizon, 1953, p 16. This distinction between the experience of nearness and distance is fully developed by the philosopher Martin Heidegger; see his *Basic Writings*, New York: Harper and Row, 1977.

12 Connors, op cit, p 61.

13 In the late 1980s the Taliesin Fellowship and FLW Foundation, in an attempt to raise funds to pay back taxes and to support the (unaccredited) FLW School at Taliesin, sold, through the Max Protetch Gallery in New York, numerous important early sketches by Wright. Among these were these four earliest design perspectives; sketchy and faint, in coloured pencils executed by Wright himself, we could see the design emerging in these drawings, not yet perfected, but in process – a rare moment indeed. Unfortunately, these four drawings are no longer available for study, having been purchased for more than $40,000 by private collectors. The FLW Foundation claimed these were 'unimportant', but what they apparently meant was they were design sketches, as they held onto the finished renderings which were generally not from Wright's hand, letting the far more important design sketches be sold. This was a serious failure on the part of the Taliesin Fellowship and FLW Foundation, which is charged with preserving, not selling off, Wright's drawings.

14 Wright, *Frank Lloyd Wright: On Architecture*, ed F Gutheim, New York: Grosset and Dunlap, 1941, p 232.

15 Wright, *In the Cause of Architecture* (1908), p 61. This is quoted in Connors' insightful study of the Robie House, op cit, where he finds three precedents within Wright's own work for the Robie House – for which again we have no surviving sketch studies.

16 Hoffmann, op cit, p 73.

17 Connors, op cit, p 61.

18 Documented and analyzed in Paul Laseau and James Tice, *Frank Lloyd Wright: Between Principle and Form*, New York: Van Nostrand Reinhold, 1992, p 34. Werner Seligmann has written an essay giving a full analysis of Fallingwater and its relation to the earlier Prairie Houses; we can only hope that this important work will one day be published.

19 One such incident, that of Wright's having holes cut in the balcony of the Robie House, is detailed by Joseph Connors, op cit, p 26.

20 This almost theatrical ability of Wright to choreograph the construction process towards his own ends is perhaps best seen in the famous sequence of structural tests he agreed to allow to be performed by the sceptical state engineers and building inspectors on the innovative 'mushroom' columns of the Johnson Wax Administration Building; see Jonathan Lipman, *Frank Lloyd Wright and the Johnson Wax Buildings*,New York: Rizzoli, 1986, pp 59–62.

21 Hoffmann, op cit, p 21.

22 Hoffmann, op cit, p 24.

23 Hoffmann, op cit, p 33.

24 Hoffmann, op cit, p 49.

25 The house and 1,543 acres of land was donated by Edgar Kaufmann, Jr, to the Western Pennsylvania Conservancy on October 29, 1963. For tours of Fallingwater, reservations and information are available from the Conservancy at PO Box R, Mill Run, Pennsylvania 15464; tel 412-329-8501.

26 Hoffmann, op cit, p 6.

27 Beautifully documented in photographs by Henry Hamilton Bennett and written about in Thomas Beeby, 'Wright and Landscape: A Mythical Interpretation', *The Nature of Frank Lloyd Wright*, ed Bolon, Nelson, Seidel, Chicago: University of Chicago Press, 1988, pp 154–72.

28 Robert P Harrison, *Forests, The Shadow of Civilization*, Chicago: Chicago University Press, 1992, p 232. Harrison's insightful discussion of Fallingwater's relation to the forest and to the landscape is far more inspiring and accurate, I believe, than the continuing efforts to see Fallingwater as yet another country house or villa in the classical tradition.

29 Harrison, op cit, p 232.

30 Frank Lloyd Wright, *The Natural House*, New York: Horizon, 1954, p 44.

31 Wright, *The Future of Architecture*, pp 321–2.

32 Wright, *In the Cause of Architecture* (1928), p 177.

33 Heidegger, 'Building Dwelling Thinking' (1951), in *Basic Writings*, op cit, p 330.

34 A phrase used by the contemporary Swiss-Italian architect Mario Botta.

35 Wright, *The Natural House*, p 58.

36 Frank Lloyd Wright, *An Autobiography*, New York: Horizon, 1977, p 164.

37 Harrison, op cit, p 233.

38 Harrison, op cit, pp 234–5. In this analysis, Harrison is indebted to Heidegger's various essays that address dwelling and architecture.

39 Hoffmann, op cit, p 27.

40 Hoffmann, op cit, p 39.

41 John Dewey, *Art as Experience* (1932), New York: Putnam's, 1980, p 237.

42 Hoffmann, op cit, p 56.

43 Wright, *An Autobiography*, p 166.

44 Categories necessary for a sense of dwelling to unfold, according to the theory of landscape proposed by Jay Appleton in his *The Experience of Landscape* and extensively utilized by Grant Hildebrandt in his *The Wright Space: Pattern and Meaning in Frank Lloyd Wright's Houses*, Seattle: University of Washington Press, 1991.

45 Wright, *An Autobiography*, p 169.

46 Dewey, op cit, p 213.

47 Hoffmann, op cit, p 92.

48 Hoffmann, op cit, p 92.

49 Hoffmann, op cit, p 92.

50 Connors, op cit, p 65.

51 Bachelard, *L'Expérience de l'espace dans la physique contemporaine*, quoted in Mary McAllester Jones, *Gaston Bachelard, Subversive Humanist*, Madison: University of Wisconsin Press, 1991, p 3.

52 Frank Lloyd Wright, *An American Architecture*, ed Edgar Kaufmann, Jr, New York: Horizon, 1955, p 61.

Chronology

1913
Kaufmann's Department Store leases Bear Run property.

1933
Edgar and Lillian Kaufmann assume ownership of Bear Run property.

October 1934
Edgar Kaufmann, Jr joins Taliesin Fellowship.

November 1934
Wright visits Bear Run site.

September 1935
Wright makes design drawings as Kaufmann drives to Taliesin.

December 1935
Rock quarry opened on site, test wall construction begins.

March 1936
Final working drawings completed by Wright.

April 1936
Construction begins on bridge and main house.

August 1936
Concrete slab poured for main floor.

October 1937
Construction on main house completed.

October 1939
Construction completed on guest house, servants' quarters and garage.

October 1963
Fallingwater and 1,543 acres donated to the Western Pennsylvania Conservancy by Edgar Kaufmann, Jr.

1979
Visitor centre built on Fallingwater site; 70,000 visitors annually.

Statistics

Location
Bear Run (stream), between Mill Run and Ohiopyle, Pennsylvania.

Area
Area of site: 1,635 acres in 1933, 1,914 acres at largest, 1,543 acres in 1963.
Area of house: 2,885 square feet (enclosed), 2,445 square feet (terraces).

Cost
$75,000 for house (1937 rates).
$22,000 for later finishing and furnishing.
$50,000 for servants' quarters, garage and guest house (1939).

Credits

Client
Edgar and Lillian Kaufmann

Architect
Frank Lloyd Wright

Project Engineers (Wright)
Mendel Glickman and William Wesley Peters

Supervising Apprentices (Wright)
Bob Mosher and Edgar Tafel

Contractor
Walter J Hall

Current Owner
Western Pennsylvania Conservancy (see also Note 25)

Bibliography

Abercrombie, Stanley, 'When a House Becomes a Museum', *AIA Journal* LXX (August 1981), pp 54–57.

Ackerman, James, *The Villa: Form and Ideology of Country Houses*. Princeton University Press, Princeton, 1990.

Apostolo, Robert, 'The Origins of Fallingwater', *Frames, Porte and Finestre* No 41 (December 1992), p 64.
'Architecture and Setting: Fallingwater, Bear Run, Frank Lloyd Wright', *Toshi jutaku* (November 1985).
'Art: Frank Lloyd Wright', *Time* XXXI (17 January 1938), p 53. (Fallingwater drawing on cover behind Wright).
10 Twentieth Century Houses. Exhibition by John Miller, Arts Council of Great Britain, 1980, pp 16–17.

Blanc, Alan, 'Forty Years On: Fallingwater, Frank Lloyd Wright's Most Famous House', *Building Design* No. 399 (9 June 1978), p 24.

Bolon, C, Nelson, R, and **Seidel, L** (ed), *The Nature of Frank Lloyd Wright*. Chicago University Press, Chicago, 1988.

Brownell, Baker and **Wright, Frank Lloyd**, *Architecture and Modern Life*. Harper and Brothers, New York, 1937. (Construction photographs.)

Connors, Joseph, *The Robie House of Frank Lloyd Wright*. University of Chicago Press, Chicago, 1984.

Donohue, Judith, 'Fixing Fallingwater's Flaws', *Architecture* (November 1989), pp 99–101.

Engel, Martin, 'The Ambiguity of Frank Lloyd Wright: Fallingwater', *Charette* XLIV (April 1964), pp 17–18.

Fallingwater and Edgar Kaufmann, Jr, Proceedings, Temple Hoyne Buell Center for the Study of American Architecture, Columbia University, New York, 1986.

'Fallingwater Saved Before It Is Imperiled: Kaufmann Makes Gift of House at Bear Run', *Architectural Record* CXXXIV (October 1963), p 24.

'Fallingwater, een landhuis van Frank Lloyd Wright', *Bouwkundig Weekblad Architectura* LIX (23 April 1938), pp 137–8.

'Fallingwater: Kaufmann House, Pennsylvania, Frank Lloyd Wright', *Kokusai Kentiku* XIV (April 1938), pp 149–56.

'Fallingwater', vivenda en Pensilvania, arq. Frank Lloyd Wright', *Neustra Arquitectura* (October 1938), pp 336–45.

Frampton, Kenneth, '1936: Frank Lloyd Wright: Fallingwater, Bear Run, Pennsylvania, USA', *Modern Architecture, 1851–1945.* Rizzoli, New York, 1981, pp 398–399.

Frank Lloyd Wright's Fallingwater. Western Pennsylvania Conservancy, Pittsburg, 1988.

'Fallingwater, Bear Run, Pennsylvania, 1935', *Architecture + Urbanism* (September 1989).

Futagawa, Yokio (ed) and **Pfeiffer, Bruce B**, *Frank Lloyd Wright Selected Houses 4: Fallingwater.* ADA Edita, Tokyo, 1990.

Futagawa, Yokio (ed) and **Pfeiffer, Bruce B**, *Frank Lloyd Wright, Monograph 1924–1936.* ADA Edita, Tokyo, 1985.

Futagawa, Yokio (photographer) and **Rudolph, Paul** (text), *Frank Lloyd Wright: Kaufmann House, 'Fallingwater', Bear Run, Pennsylvania, 1936.* ADA Edita, Tokyo, 1970.

Futagawa, Yokio (ed), *Houses by Frank Lloyd Wright 2.* ADA Edita, Tokyo, 1975.

Gill, Brendan, *Many Masks: A Life of Frank Lloyd Wright .* Putnam's, New York, 1987.

Gill, Brendan, 'Edgar Kaufmann, Jr: Secrets of Fallingwater', *Architectural Digest* (March 1990), pp 50–64.

Hamlin, Talbot, 'F L W – An Analysis', *Pencil Points* XIX (March 1938), pp 137–44.

Harrison, Robert P., 'Fallingwater', *Forests: The Shadow of Civilization.* Chicago University Press, Chicago, 1992, pp 232–237.

Hildebrandt, Grant, *The Wright Space: Pattern and Meaning in Frank Lloyd Wright's Houses.* University of Washington Press, Seattle, 1991.

Hill, John deKoven, 'The Poetry of Structure', *House Beautiful* XCVIII (November 1955), pp 246–7, 348–50.

Hitchcock, Henry-Russell, *In the Nature of Materials; 1887–1941, The Buildings of Frank Lloyd Wright.* Duell, Sloan and Pierce, New York, 1941.

Hoesli, Bernhard, 'Frank Lloyd Wright: Fallingwater', *Architecture + Urbanism* No 118 (July 1980), pp 155–66.

Hoffmann, Donald, *Frank Lloyd Wright's Fallingwater: The House and Its History.* Dover, New York, 1978, 1993 (new colour photography). (Most comprehensive and accurate history of design and construction).

'A House of Leaves: The Poetry of Fallingwater', *Charette* XLIV (April 1964), pp 13–16.

'The Impact of Genius: Fallingwater, 1936', *House Beautiful* (November 1986).

Izzo, Alberto and **Gubitosi, Camillo**, (ed), *Frank Lloyd Wright: Drawings, 1887–1959.* Centro Di, Firenze, 1981.

Johnson, Donald Leslie, *Frank Lloyd Wright versus America: The 1930s.* MIT Press, Cambridge, 1990.

Kaufmann, Jr, Edward, *9 Commentaries on Frank Lloyd Wright.* MIT Press, Cambridge, 1989.

Kaufmann, Jr, Edward, 'How Right was Wright', *House and Garden* (August 1986).

Kaufmann, Jr, Edward, 'The House on the Waterfall', *Writings on Wright.* H Allen Brooks, (ed), MIT Press, Cambridge, 1981, pp 69–72.

Kaufmann, Jr, Edward, *Fallingwater: A Frank Lloyd Wright Country House.* Abbeville Press, New York, 1986. (First hand account by son of owner, later a scholar on Wright).

Kaufmann, Jr, Edward, *Fallingwater.* Architectural Press, London, 1986.

Kaufmann, Jr, Edward, 'Frank Lloyd Wright's Fallingwater 25 Years After', *Architettura* VII (August 1962), pp 222–80.

Kaufmann, Jr, Edward, 'Fallingwater at 50', *Interior Design* (July 1986).

Laseau, Paul and **Tice, James**, *Frank Lloyd Wright: Between Principle and Form.* Van Nostrand Reinhold, New York, 1992.

Levine, Neil, 'Frank Lloyd Wright's Diagonal Planning', *In Search of Modern Architecture: A Tribute to Henry Russell Hitchcock.* MIT Press, Cambridge, 1982.

Lind, Carla, *The Wright Style: Recreating the Spirit of Frank Lloyd Wright.* Simon and Schuster, New York, 1992.

Louchheim, Aline Bernstein, 'Frank Lloyd Wright Talks of His Art', *New York Times Magazine* (October 4, 1953), p 27.

McCarter, Robert, (ed), *Frank Lloyd Wright: A Primer on Architectural Principles.* Princeton Architectural Press, New York, 1991.

McCarter, Robert, 'Woven Space, Anchored Place: The Houses of Frank Lloyd Wright, 1935–1959', *GA Houses* 43, 1994.

Mock, Elizabeth, (ed) and Goodwin, Philip, *Built in USA Since 1932.* Museum of Modern Art, New York, 1945.

Mumford, Lewis, 'The Skyline – At Home, Indoors and Out', *The New Yorker* XII (12 February 1938), p 31.

Museum of Modern Art, *A New House by Frank Lloyd Wright on Bear Run, Pennsylvania.* MOMA, New York, 1938.

'New Visitors' Center Completed at Fallingwater', *Frank Lloyd Wright Newsletter* IV, No.2, (1981), p 18.

'One Hundred Years of Significant Building, 9: Houses Since 1907', *Architectural Record* CXXI (February 1957), pp 199–206.

Patterson, Augusta Owen, 'Three Modern Houses, No. 3: Owner, Edgar Kaufmann, Pittsburgh; Architect, Frank Lloyd Wright', *Town and Country* XCIII (February 1938), pp 64–5, 104.

Peterson, Jay, 'Nature's Architect', *New Masses* XXVI (8 February 1938), pp 29–30.

Plummer, Henry, *The Potential House. Architecture + Urbanism*, Tokyo (September 1989), pp 128–39.

Purves, Alexander, 'This goodly frame, the Earth', *Perspecta* (1989), pp 178–201.

Putzel, Max, 'A House That Straddles a Waterfall', *St. Louis Post-Dispatch* Sunday Magazine (March 21, 1937), pp 1–7.

Riecken, Andrea, 'Cinqueta anos da Casa da Cascata, s'imbolo do modernismo americano', *Projecto* (July 1987), pp 74–8.

Sainz, Jorge, 'El sueño cristalizado: Fallingwater a gusto de todos', *A and V* (1987), pp 56–8.

Saltz, Jerry, 'I Could Live Here', *Arts Magazine* (March 1989), pp 23–4.

Scully, Vincent, *Frank Lloyd Wright.* George Braziller, New York, 1960.

Smith, Norris Kelly, *Frank Lloyd Wright, A Study in Architectural Content.* Prentice-Hall, Englewood Cliffs, NJ, 1979.

Sorkin, Michael, 'Fallingwater at Fifty', *Connoisseur* (August 1986).

Storrer, William, *The Architecture of Frank Lloyd Wright: A Complete Catalog.* MIT Press, Cambridge, 1974, 1978.

Tafel, Edgar, *Apprentice to Genius: Years with Frank Lloyd Wright.* Dover, New York, 1979, 1985.

'Wright's Masterpiece Preserved', *Interiors* CXXII (October 1963), p 12.

'Wright's Newest', *Art Digest* XII (1 February 1938), p 13.

Wright, Frank Lloyd, 'Frank Lloyd Wright', *Architectural Forum* LXVIII (January 1938), pp 36–47. (Issue written and designed by Wright).

Wright, Frank Lloyd, *In the Cause of Architecture.* F. Gutheim, (ed), reprint of *Architectural Record* essays. McGraw-Hill, New York, 1975.

Wright, Frank Lloyd, *Frank Lloyd Wright: On Architecture.* F. Gutheim (ed), Grosset and Dunlap, New York, 1941.

Wright, Frank Lloyd, *Drawings for a Living Architecture.* Horizon Press, New York, 1959.

Wright, Frank Lloyd, *Frank Lloyd Wright: Writings and Buildings.* Kaufmann, Jr, E and Raeburn, B (ed), Horizon Press, New York, 1960.

Wright, Frank Lloyd, *An Autobiography.* Duell, Sloan and Pierce, New York, 1943.

Zevi, Bruno and **Kaufmann, Edgar, Jr**, *La Casa sulla Cascata di F. Ll. Wright: Frank Lloyd Wright's Fallingwater.* ET/AS Kompass, Milano, 1963.

Zevi, Bruno, 'Il vaticinio del Riegl e la Casa sulla Cascata', *Architettura* VIII (August 1962), pp 218–21.

Alvar Aalto
Villa Mairea
Noormarkku 1937–9

Richard Weston

Photography
Rauno Träskelin; cover detail
also by Rauno Träskelin
Drawings
Darren Stewart Capel

Alvar Aalto and the National Romantic movement

Finland achieved independence as recently as 1917, following the Russian October Revolution. For 800 years it had been part of the Swedish empire and in 1809, following Sweden's defeat by the armies of Napoleon Bonaparte and Czar Nicholas I, was declared a grand-duchy of Russia. During the latter part of the 19th century a vigorous nationalist movement opposed to Russian rule became the focus of cultural activity, leading around the turn of the century to what is known as the National Romantic movement. Artists, writers, composers and architects sought the roots of authentic Finnish culture in medieval stone churches and castles, vernacular artefacts and timber buildings, and above all in the landscape of forests and lakes. In deliberate contrast to the increasingly opulent culture of the ruling élite, a life of 'noble poverty' lived close to nature became an ideal for many, and the painter Akseli Gallen-Kallela led the movement back to nature by building his studio-home 'Kalela' (1894–95), **1**, on the remote shores of Lake Ruovesi. His example was followed by other artists, including most notably the composer Sibelius, who became part of an artistic community which developed around Lake Tuusula, rather more conveniently located some 20 miles north of Helsinki.

The leading architects of the National Romantic movement, Herman Gesellius, Armas Lindgren and Eliel Saarinen, built their studio-home 'Hvitträsk', **2**, on a wooded site above Lake Vitträsk, which combined the requisite feeling of remoteness with a tolerable proximity to the capital. Its design drew freely on the English Arts and Crafts, American Shingle Style and Viennese *Jugendstil*, and also incorporated elements derived from vernacular traditions, ranging from log construction (later largely concealed by shingles) to vaulted castle-like rooms, **3**. Hvitträsk exemplified the movement's ideals of the home as a 'total work of art' and of architecture as an expression of national identity, ideals to which Alvar Aalto returned in the 1930s and of which he was to give consummate expression in the design of the Villa Mairea.

Alvar Aalto was born in 1898 and after studying in Helsinki established his own office in Jyväskylä, where he had been brought up. Early projects such as the Workers' Club in Jyväskylä of 1923, **4**, and the Civil Defence Corps building in Seinäjoki (1924–29), **5**, were designed in the Nordic Classical style, but by 1928 Aalto had made the transition to Modernism, as demonstrated in the Turun Sanomat newspaper offices in Turku, **6**, completed that year and clearly indebted to the work of Le Corbusier. The Paimio Sanatorium (1928–33), **7**, established Aalto's international reputation as a master of the new architecture and also contained hints, in details such as the free-form entrance canopy, of his efforts to give a regional inflection to an avowedly international style. In his own house (1934–36), in Munkkiniemi, the western extension of Helsinki, **8**, and in the Finnish Pavilion at the Paris World Fair of 1937, the use of natural materials such as timber boarding and overtly hand-crafted details confirm Aalto's determination to create a Finnish interpretation of Modernism comparable to the nationalist version of *Jugendstil* developed at the beginning of the century. The commission for the Villa Mairea offered him the ideal opportunity to explore further the potential of this approach.

The clients: Harry and Maire Gullichsen

The Villa Mairea was designed for Harry and Maire Gullichsen, to whom Aalto was introduced in 1935 by Nils-Gustav Hahl, who was keen to promote his bent-wood furniture designs. Maire, after whom the house was named, was the daughter of Walter Ahlström, director of the vast Ahlström timber and paper company. She studied painting in Paris during the early 1920s and in 1928 married the businessman Harry Gullichsen, who four years later became managing director of the Ahlström company. Maire and Hahl had the idea of founding an avant-garde art gallery in Helsinki to act as a focus of progressive culture, and in due course this became 'Artek', now world-famous as manufacturers and distributors of Aalto's furniture and glassware, **9**. The Gullichsens

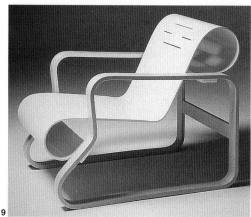

and their circle believed in the possibility of a social utopia based on reason and technological progress, and in Alvar Aalto found a designer who shared their ideals and could give them convincing architectural expression. Aalto and his first wife Aino undertook various projects for the Ahlström company, including workers' housing, social facilities, and the celebrated Sunila Plant, completed in 1939, but it was in the Villa Mairea itself that the character of their utopian vision was demonstrated most fully.

The villa was the third major house built with Ahlström money. In 1877 the founder of the company, Maire's grandfather Antti Ahlström, had built an imposing wooden house as the family residence in Noormarkku, a village a few miles inland from the town of Pori on Finland's west coast; at the turn of the century her father, Walter, commissioned an art nouveau house on a nearby site. As Aalto's biographer Göran Schildt has pointed out, each house was representative of the values of their owners and of their time: the first an expression of semi-feudal authority organized around a highly formalized style of living, the latter underlining 'the domestic happiness afforded by solid riches, with comfortable rooms, cosy furniture and luxurious, well-tended garden grounds'.[1] The new villa – to be used as a summer house, a form of retreat to nature traditional in Finland – was intended to express the aspirations of the new generation and of the Gullichsens' vision

of 'the good life' which they believed industrialization would eventually make available to the majority in the newly-independent social democratic state.

Social concerns

Such aspirations were hardly new. In the aftermath of the First World War, modern architects had been preoccupied with the problems of mass-housing, and Le Corbusier, amongst others, envisaged the harnessing of industrialized production as a means of solving the severe housing shortages – hence his obsession with generalized types: an early prototype house was named 'Citrohan'[2], **10**, suggesting that it was to be mass-produced like Citroën cars. In Finland, workers' housing was also a major concern during the 1920s: industrial modernization had come late and there was massive migration from the countryside to the cities. The necessary economic stringency coincided happily with the ascetic aesthetic ideals of the Nordic Classical style;[3] one of the most notable achievements of the period was the industrialized construction of Puu-Käpylä, **11**, a workers' housing estate on the northern outskirts of Helsinki designed by Martti Välikangas. Following his conversion to Modernism, Aalto experimented with low-cost housing in his Standard Apartment Block, **12**, constructed in Turku in 1929, and the following year wrote an article on 'The Dwelling as a Problem' in which he attempted to 'get at the scien-

tific conditions for the standard dwelling in society'.[4]

Despite his initial enthusiasm, Aalto soon distanced himself from the more technocratic proponents of Modernism and advocated nature as a model for architectural standardization. Lecturing in Oslo in 1938, for example, he argued that 'in opposition to the view that sees established forms and uniformity as the only way to achieve architectural harmony and successfully controlled building techniques, I have tried… to emphasize that architecture's inner nature is a fluctuation and a development suggestive of natural organic life'.[5]

Although the Villa Mairea was to be a luxurious house, apparently worlds apart from the problems of mass-housing, Aalto and his clients were eager to see in it a model of wide relevance. Introducing its presentation in the Society of Finnish Architects' magazine *Arkkitehti*, Aalto argued that there need not be any conflict between the mass-produced small dwelling and the privately commissioned residence. The latter, he suggested, could be used as 'a kind of experimental laboratory, where one can realize that which is not possible for the present mass production, but out of which these experimental cases spread gradually… to become an objective available for everyone'.[6] In retrospect this may seem politically naive, but one should not doubt the conviction with which such views were held at the time.

11

10

12

13

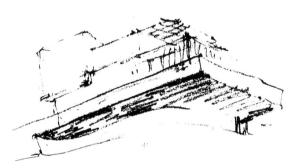

14

Initial ideas

Aalto began work on the Villa towards the end of 1937, and was given an almost free hand by his clients: 'We told him that he should regard it as an experimental house; if it didn't work out, we wouldn't blame him for it', Maire Gullichsen recalled. His first proposal was a rustic hut modelled on vernacular farmhouses, which prompted Maire to exclaim 'Well, we asked you to make something Finnish but in the spirit of today'.[7] Early in 1938, however, inspiration came from a radically different source, namely Frank Lloyd Wright's 'Fallingwater', 13, which had just received international acclaim thanks to an exhibition at the Museum of Modern Art in New York and publication in *Life* and *Time* magazines as well as in architectural journals. Such was Aalto's enthusiasm for the design, Schildt tells us,[8] that he tried to persuade the Gullichsens to build their home over a stream on Ahlström land a few miles out of Noormarkku!

The influence of Fallingwater is evident in several sheets of studies, 14, 15, which show boldly cantilevered balconies and an undulating basement storey intended as a substitute for the natural forms of the stream and rocks. In later sketches, the free-form basement appears as an upper-floor studio whose serpentine wall is sunk into a one-and-a-half storey entrance hall, forming a drop-ceiling around the fire. The undulating, wave-like form was already established as a leitmotiv of Aalto's work: it was familiar from the vases designed for the Savoy restaurant and featured prominently in the second-prize-winning entry for the Finnish Pavilion at the Paris World Fair of 1937, named 'Tsit Tsit Pum', 16. (Aalto won first prize with a different design and, never one to waste a good idea, used a vast sinuous partition as the primary spatial device of his masterly design for the New York Fair of 1939.) The free forms of nature were seen as symbols of human freedom, and as early as 1926 Aalto remarked that the 'curving, living, unpredictable line which runs in dimensions unknown to mathematicians, is for me the incarnation of everything that forms a contrast in the modern world between brutal mechanicalness and religious beauty in life'.[9] The fact that the Finnish word *aalto* means 'wave' doubtless added a certain piquancy to his attraction to the motif.

Throughout his early studies for the Villa, Aalto envisaged an L-shaped plan similar to that of his own house in Munkkiniemi (1934–36), 17. There, the 'L' served to distinguish between the house proper and the integral studio; in Mairea it separates the family accommodation from that of the servants and guests, and forms two sides of a courtyard/garden variously enclosed by combinations of walls, fences, trellises and the wooden sauna. Demetri Porphyrios[10] has pointed out that this plan form is common amongst Scandinavian aristocratic

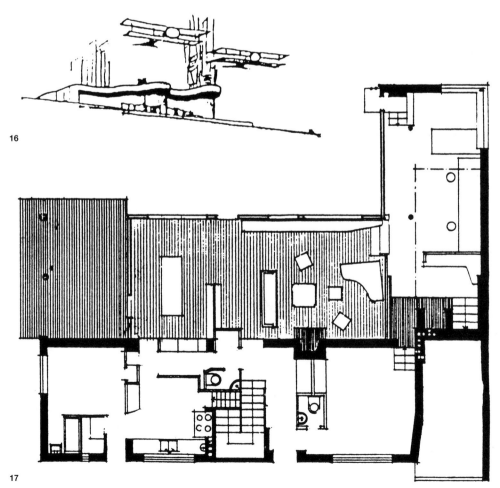

16

17

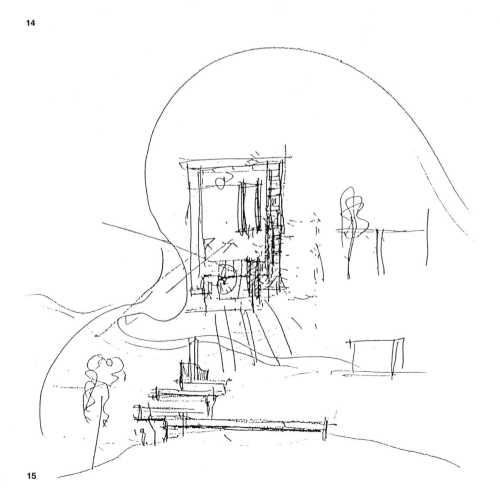

15

residences; it was also used, for example, by Gunnar Asplund in his celebrated Snellman house of 1919. Although Aalto's clients had asked for an 'experimental' house, it is significant that he first envisaged it as a reversion to a vernacular form, and then as a variant on a familiar plan type: in embodying a vision of the future Aalto is at pains to endow the dwelling with strong memories of the past.

The 'Proto-Mairea'

In the early spring of 1938 the Gullichsens approved a design which Schildt has called the Proto-Mairea, and on the basis of which construction began in the summer. The plan, **18**, established the basic disposition of accommodation found in the finished house, with the dining room situated in the corner between the family rooms and the servant wing, and the bedrooms and Maire's studio upstairs, the latter originally expressed as a free-form curve in elevation, **19**, rather than plan. Aalto's analysis of the activities to be accommodated produced a schedule of reception rooms which included an entrance hall with open fireplace, living room, gentlemen's room, ladies' room, library, music-room, winter garden, table tennis room and art gallery.[11] It reads more like the programme for a Victorian country house than a demonstration of the social-democratic dwelling of the future, and Aalto was far from satisfied with the design. A young Swiss student

working in his office at the time recalls that he used to scold the model like a naughty dog, explaining to her that 'those people don't need so many rooms'.[12]

After the foundations had been excavated Aalto had a new idea and was able to persuade his clients to accept a radical redesign in which only the plan footprint and servant wing remained more or less intact. The basement was greatly reduced in area, and the main entrance moved from its curious position at the side and rear to a much more obvious location in front of the dining room. Maire's studio was re-positioned to occupy the place above the former entrance canopy, whose shape it echoes, and the various reception rooms were accommodated in a large 14 metre-square space. The separate art gallery was removed and its place taken by the sauna, which nestled against a low L-shaped stone wall, the remainder of the original wall and trellis being replaced by a short fence and earth mound.

Harry Gullichsen's only objection to the revised design was the lack of a separate library where he could hold confidential business meetings, for which Aalto proposed a small room screened by movable shelving units which did not reach the ceiling, **20**; he suggested that these units could also be used for storing Maire's art collection – an idea which, he pointed out, should be 'socially supportable as it could be realized in a small, even

single room, dwelling' where the inhabitant has 'a personal relationship to the phenomena of art'.[13] Not surprisingly this arrangement did not offer the necessary acoustic privacy and the shelving units were permanently sited (although not actually fixed), with one angled to suggest frozen movement; the gap under the ceiling was filled with an undulating glazed screen.

The final design: ground floor

Although the revised plan followed the existing foundations, the transformation achieved a compression and coherence in the spatial organization which had been almost entirely lacking in the 'Proto-Mairea'. The entrance opens into a small, top-lit lobby, from which another door straight ahead leads into an open hall positioned four steps below the main level. One enters on axis with the dining table beyond, but the axiality is undermined by the asymmetry of a screen of wooden poles and a free-standing, angled wall which together define an informal ante-room between the living room and dining room. The angle of the low wall is set from the corner of the white-plastered fireplace diagonally opposite, which becomes the natural centre of attention as one ascends the steps into the living room, **21**. Similar diagonal relationships are established between Harry Gullichsen's private library/study and the 'winter garden' (which Maire used for

23

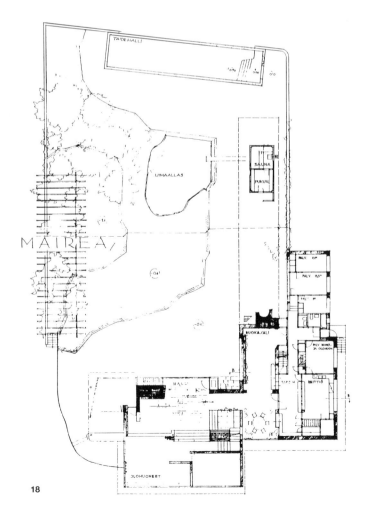

18

20

22

21

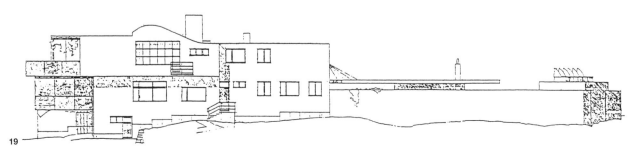

19

flower arranging and from which a stair leads directly up into her studio), and between the main staircase and open sun-lit part of the living room into which your eye is drawn as you emerge from behind the vertical poles which screen the stairs, **22**.

The open living room is planned around a rectilinear structural grid whose dimensions are adjusted to suit the disposition of rooms above, in contrast to the conventional Modernist practice exemplified by the work of Le Corbusier and Mies van der Rohe, in which the structural grid was conceived as a regular counterpoint to the independent spatial disposition of the 'free plan'. Aalto, by contrast, does everything he can to avoid what he calls 'artificial architectural rhythms in the building':[14] not only does he vary the dimensions of the grid in both directions, but the circular steel columns are randomly doubled and, in one case, tripled, clad with wooden strips or bound with rattan, **23**, and, in the library, one of the three columns is arbitrarily changed to concrete (early sketches also show it as free-form in plan). Aalto is at such pains to subvert any clear geometric reading of the structural and spatial organization that it comes as something of a surprise to discover that the whole plan is in fact regulated by a series of squares.

Although this geometry contributes to the formal discipline which underpins the episodic spatial composition – and is emblematic of an 'ideal' house – it is only in the dining room, **24**, that one can sense directly the underlying order. The room itself is a double-square in plan, and the triple-square of the service block is centred on it: the formality is entirely appropriate to the activity of dining and entertaining and can be interpreted, as Klaus Herdeg has argued,[15] as an architectural embodiment of the social traditions of the bourgeois family. Harry Gullichsen, as head of the household, occupied the head of the table facing towards the entrance. From there he could see along the axis to the entrance and beyond into the pine forest through the clerestorey windows above the vestibule, and also diagonally through the entire living room. Mrs Gullichsen would occupy the seat at the opposite end of the table, conveniently close to the servery and kitchen, from where, as Herdeg writes, she 'can contemplate her husband silhouetted against the dining room's asymmetrical fireplace, while through the window she can see the sauna, the pool, the garden court, and the pine forest – things natural or traditional. Most of these views the father would only see reflected in an artifice: the living room windows'.[16]

The flat roof of the dining room is extended to form a covered terrace, **25**, which connects with the irregular roof of the small timber sauna. The terrace is served by a fire which backs up against the fireplace in the dining room, and over which a rustic stone staircase rises to the wooden deck on the roof. The angle of the stairs determines the line of the plaster which rises diagonally across the fire to level out over the door. The same angle is continued outside in the flue which connects at first-floor level into the service wing – a typical example of the rigorous formal integration which underlies Aalto's at times seemingly wilful manipulation of form. The rectangular pier at the end of the terrace affords another example. Viewed in isolation this seems to be simply another instance of Aalto's desire to break the 'artificial rhythms' established by a regular grid, akin to the doubling and tripling of columns in the living room. But it also acts as a visual and formal termination to the implied band of secondary circulation which runs through the door between dining room and terrace, past the servery and on to the narrow steps adjacent to the angled wall which defines the entrance hall.

The first floor

By comparison with the sophisticated spatial composition of the ground floor, the first floor is a relatively straightforward assemblage of private rooms. The main stair arrives in an intimate upper hall, with its own fireplace placed directly above that below, **26**. Mr and Mrs Gullichsen's bedrooms are paired either side of an *en suite* bathroom and are entered under a slightly dropped ceiling, which houses vents for conditioned air and terminates in a familiar serpentine line. The three children's bedrooms open onto a large circulation/play space, fitted with wall bars for exercise, **27**. Their windows are obliquely projecting bays, **28**, which read almost as objects on the facade, rather than openings in it, and are angled to address the line of approach to the main door. The guest bedrooms are disposed along a single-banked corridor and look out north-east into the forest; the corridor is lined with full-height cupboards and presents a blank wall to the family's private garden.

Aalto's treatment of space

In his description of the Villa, Aalto remarks somewhat obscurely that 'the formal concept associated with the architecture of this special building... includes a deliberate connection to modern painting which gives the building and the home a deeper and basically more human substance'.[17] This link may in part have been prompted by Maire Gullichsen's personal involvement with modern art, both as a student painter and collector, but, as Göran Schildt has pointed out, painting had been a decisive influence in the formation of Aalto's ideas – 'But it all began in painting' was a frequent remark.[18] This 'connection to modern painting' can be seen in two related but distinct ways: firstly, in Aalto's conception of interior space, indebted originally to Cézanne; and secondly, in his painterly as opposed

24

26

25

27

to architectonic handling of form.

What Aalto discovered in Cézanne, Schildt argues, was a treatment of space quite unlike that in paintings governed by the conventions of linear perspective dominant in Western painting since the Renaissance: 'If we look at a painting by Cézanne… we see how the space grows directly out of the forms placed on the canvas; individual elements with volume spread out towards the sides from an intensely modulated central zone. There is no abstract space here, merely concrete relations between forms and volumes, surfaces forming partly overlapping solids, creating an impression of space which is neither uniform nor unambiguously coherent… Aalto's great discovery was that architectural interiors can be treated in the same way.'[19] The idea of rendering interior space as a kind of 'outside inside' was a favourite theme of 1920s Classicism in Scandinavia – Asplund's Skandia Cinema in Stockholm, for example, was decked out to represent an Italian piazza under the deep blue southern sky, and Aalto employed a similar concept in the foyer of his Workers' Club in Jyväskylä of 1923, in which the semi-circular wall of the theatre could be interpreted as the outside of an apse. In various projects of the 1930s Aalto developed this into an architectural evocation of the open space of nature, and in particular the characteristic 'forest space' of Finland.[20] This idea appears in 1936 in the 'Tsit Tsit Pum' entry for the Paris World Fair competition, in which columns and flags are deployed as architectural counterparts of trees, and a complex, episodic space is conjured from a freely organized series of volumes, forms and levels. Aalto returned to the theme, albeit in a much more compressed and abstracted form, in the masterly New York Pavilion of 1938–39, and it was to prove one of the hallmarks of his handling of interior space throughout his subsequent career.

This conception of 'forest space' provides a key to understanding Aalto's intentions in the Villa Mairea. Walking around the living room, **29**, one experiences neither the containment of traditional interiors, nor the open 'flowing space' of modern architecture, but something very much akin to the feeling of wandering through a forest in which spaces seem to form and re-form around you: in a forest, the individual feels himself to be the moving centre of its spaces. For Aalto such 'forest spaces' provided both a means of 'naturalizing' his architecture and also of achieving a 'democratic', non-hierarchical organization conceived around 'the small man' for whom he wished to build.

In the Villa, Aalto achieves this spatial quality in several ways: by the varied handling of the perimeter, which ranges from solid, to part-glazed, to the full-height sliding glass screen between the fireplace and main stair; by destroying the square of the living room through the intrusion of the volumes of the garden room and library (the surfaces of the former read as the 'exteriors' of the room behind rather than as bounding planes of the living room itself, whilst the latter is defined by the object-like storage units which exist 'in' the space); by counterpointing the continuous pine-strip suspended ceiling (pierced with 52,000 holes to admit conditioned air) with the varied materials and textures of the floor. The sequence from red slate in the entrance, through ceramic tiles to white beech, with natural stone in the garden room and around the fireplace, marks out the transition from outdoors to indoors, from nature to domesticity; and finally, by a series of subtle but unmistakable formal analogies with landscape.

Most obvious are the tree-like poles which screen the stair and help separate the ante-space to the dining room from the entrance below, **30**. These poles rhyme with the steel columns, further undermining any suggestion of 'artificial architectural rhythms' to which the structural grid might give rise, and absorbing the structure into the overall free – 'natural' – rhythmic development of the space. The columns themselves, as we noted above, are variously bound with rattan or partially clad with timber strips. The wrapping and cladding serve to 'naturalize' and 'humanize' the standard industrial products, rendering them richly tactile objects, and can also be seen as evoking memories of both Classical and natural forms. The timber cladding can be interpreted as both an allusion to the fluting of Doric columns and as an evocation of the texture of bark – a double-reading which Aalto frequently exploited, notably with his later tile claddings. The wrapped columns can similarly be read as referring to the Classical tripartite division into base, shaft and capital; the rattan seen against the black paint offers a vivid abstraction of the trunks of mature pine trees on which the dark outer bark peels away to reveal the golden layer below.

Allusions to nature

Such evocations of natural forms and textures reinforce Aalto's 'naturalization' of the architecture of the Villa – their 'fluctuation' is indeed 'suggestive of natural organic life' – and once one recognizes the game which he is playing the possible references begin to multiply. It is tempting, for example, to see the curious, splayed double-column, **31**, which supports the studio as a twin-stemmed silver birch tree, **32**, a familiar sight near the edges of pine forests – and just the position it occupies here, at the edge of the building and the pine-tree columns within. The white circular columns which support the deck over the covered terrace and the nearby timber columns of the sauna roof similarly become absorbed visually into the forest setting, and the sensuous moulding of

28

29

30

31

32

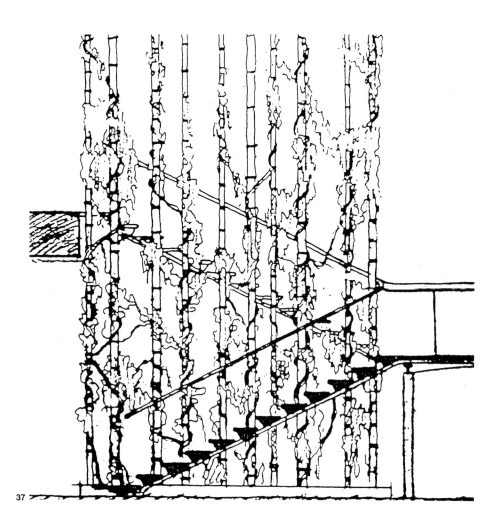

the fireplace, **33**, known in the office at the time as 'Aalto's ear',[21] recalls the forms of snow, wind-sculpted and melted by the fire – as well as being a beautiful way of resolving a potentially awkward juxtaposition of solid masonry and glass.

A further intriguing instance is provided by the glazed slot around the library. Given that Aalto wished to preserve the openness of the living room and to suggest that the partitions which define the library were notionally movable, it is surprising that he did not opt to insert a minimal glazed screen. What he did create, however, is a marvellous evocation of a horizontal 'slice' of forest, **34**, through which shafts of light suggest the familiar broken sunlight of the forest edge – just such a 'slice' of forest, incidentally, is visible between the split levels of the entrance canopy, **35**, and a similarly vivid suggestion of forest light is created in the late afternoon when the sun slants through the main staircase.

The play on natural form is introduced immediately on arrival at the house by the screen of thin timbers adjacent to the main door which evoke a forest-in-miniature, **36**, an arrangement almost certainly inspired by Japanese bamboo fences. An early sketch for the main staircase shows that Aalto originally thought of screening it with bamboo, **37**, and traces of this idea remain in the detailing which seems to echo the natural growth rings of bamboo. Aalto was a close friend of the Japanese

ambassador and his wife and they later recalled that he had a substantial collection of books on Japanese architecture.[22] The garden room, with its delicate glazed screen and Katsura-inspired shelves, and details such as the paving and stone bases to the columns under the entrance canopy, are clearly indebted to traditional Japanese architecture. The exquisitely refined sauna – most obviously the elaborated entrance transition and subdivision of the door, **38** – likewise suggest the inspiration of tea-houses, **39**.

Aalto's painterly handling of form

Having examined at some length the transformation of the modern open plan into an inner landscape evocative of the surrounding forest, we must return to consider the second aspect of the Villa's 'connection to modern painting', namely Aalto's decidedly 'painterly' handling of form. Every view of the house, **40**, presents a remarkable array of forms, colours, and textures – abstract white planes, lime-washed brickwork, weatherboarding, teak and stone cladding, assorted poles, trellises and wooden and metal railings, blue-glazed tiles, grass roofs, a spiral staircase, fragments of structure, climbing plants... Although Aalto was, as ever, less than explicit about the sources of his ideas, the inspiration for such an approach is surely to be found in Cubist painting, and in particular in the technique of *papier collé* or

37

35

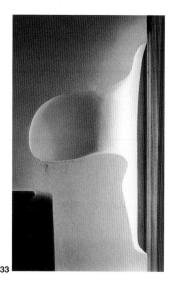

33

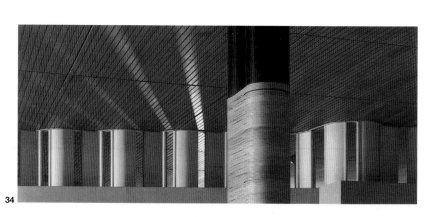

34

36

38

39

'collage' invented by Georges Braque one famous day in September 1912 when he pasted onto a canvas a strip of paper with simulated wood-graining. Fragments of sheet-music, daily papers, even a section of chair caning, soon followed in the work of Braque, Picasso and other Cubists, and it is precisely such canvases that provide the closest formal model for Aalto's radical assault on the conventional handling of architectural form. Just as the fragments chosen by the Cubists were absorbed into the formal structure of the painting but also carried with them direct associations with aspects of everyday life – the newspapers and chairs of a café, for example – so in the Villa, Aalto's fragmentary forms and surfaces operate both visually and referentially.

Glimpsed through the forest the front elevation evokes the 'white box' of an orthodox Modern house, but as one draws closer this image is overlaid and, indeed, subverted in several ways. The living room is clad in teak and stone as a mark of its importance, whilst above and behind it the studio is faced with vertical weather-boarding. At first-floor level a white staircase spirals up to the roof and a single column supports a fragment of beam with a tapering cantilever, over which is laid a timber trellis. The free-form and 'rustic' structure of the entrance canopy speak an entirely different formal language, and to their side a series of slender poles support

climbing plants and describe a serpentine line across the surface which wraps around, and thereby visually dissolves, the corner.

In the courtyard beyond, the juxtapositions are even more startling. Consider the corner of the dining room, for example, **41**. Here the white rendered volume is eroded by a seemingly random patch of blue-glazed tiles, which turn – and similarly dissolve – the corner to form the backdrop to a rough stone staircase. The handrail to the stairs is circular and of polished wood, whilst the wooden deck over the dining room has a balustrade formed of square mild-steel uprights which support timber poles, used as-found but for the removal of the bark, **42**, and directly in front of the stairs is one of the white-painted circular concrete columns which support the turf-roof over the terrace.

The sheer wealth of materials and motifs is astonishing. Although some, such as the blue tiles outside (and brickwork inside) the end wall of the dining room appear, as Juhani Pallasmaa aptly puts it, 'only once as isolated brushstrokes'[23] and carry no obvious meaning, most are carefully calculated allusions to either Finnish vernacular traditions, **43**, or to the recognized forms of architectural modernity. Amongst the former, for example, we might note the turf-roofed timber sauna and the artfully cultivated 'primitiveness' of its surrounding structure; the low stone wall around Hollold churchyard

43

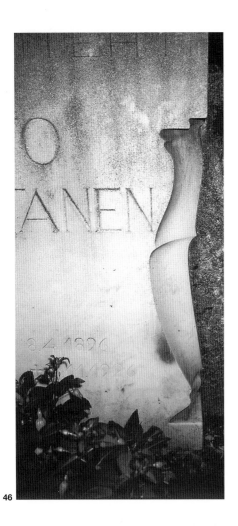

which recalls similar walls around medieval church-yards, **44**; the timber balustrade which echoes farm fences; the weather-boarding of the studio; the timber gutters; and, to cite just one more instance, the handle on the main entrance door which is a representation in brass of the natural wooden handles – straight-from-the-tree as it were – frequently found on traditional buildings. The white-plastered fireplace offers a particularly rich range of associations: it immediately recalls a vernacular form, but may also be an allusion to the sculpturally elaborate fireplace which the painter Gallen-Kallela incorporated in his studio-home 'Kalela', **45**. We noted above that the sensuous relief is suggestive of wind-sculpted snow; formally, it was probably inspired by the reliefs of Aalto's friend Hans Arp; and comparison with the gravestone, **46**, which Aalto designed for his brother-in-law, the architect Ahto Virtanen who died in 1935, may even lead one to agree with Kenneth Frampton's suggestion that it also harks back to 'the lost profiles of classical architecture'.[24]

Allusions to Modernism are similarly pervasive and range from the white surfaces of the main volumes with their substantial areas of glazing, including the obligatory full-height sliding screen (used only once or twice in fifty years!), to details such as the 'nautical' handrails, external spiral staircase and adjacent round-cornered 'ship's-door', fragments of structure, and so forth.

The painterliness of Aalto's handling of form was also inspired by Maire Gullichsen's involvement with modern art, both as student and collector, and her studio recalls the milieu of Paris by quoting from Aalto's Finnish Pavilion for the Paris World Fair of 1937. Paul Bernoulli, who worked as a site architect on the project, recalls that it was following Maire's interventions that several of the most painterly touches were included.[25] The structurally redundant angled column under the studio, for example, appeared on the early elevations but was later eliminated by the consulting engineer, only to be reinstated at Maire's insistence – Bernoulli remembers having to buy the steel tube himself, which neither connects to the beam nor bears on the foundation. Similarly the blue tiling around the end of the dining room was also introduced following discussion with Maire: at her suggestion, Aalto envisaged painting it ultramarine, like the night sky in Asplund's Skandia Cinema, but opted for the more durable tiles which had to be brought from Denmark to get the desired colour.

Tradition and modernity

The more one looks, the more subtle Aalto's play on these references becomes. The white surfaces, for example, are not the smooth render one would expect, but lime-washed brickwork more reminiscent of Mediterranean vernacular than the abstract

forms of the 'machine age' – and also more durable in the harsh Finnish climate. Similarly, the weather-boarding of the studio, **47**, which appears conventional from a distance is in fact made of subtly-profiled boards. Juxtapositions of 'traditional' and 'modern' are repeated throughout the design: the exemplarily 'modern' concrete frame of the terrace supports a timber deck and turf-roof, complete with birch-bark lining and hollowed-out-log gutter, **48**; the 'farm-fence' handrail above the dining room is supported by mild steel posts; the poles of the trellises around the service wing form miniature *De Stijl* constructions without any hint of how the timbers are joined – in marked contrast to the elaborately bound joints of the columns and beams which support the sauna roof (an idea derived from African buildings and artefacts which Aalto saw at the Brussels World Fair in 1935, and which he also used in the realized design for the Finnish Pavilion at the Fair in Paris two years later. The African examples may well also have been the inspiration for the wrapping of the steel columns in the living room).[26]

Aalto's technique of collage-composition enabled him to incorporate disparate and seemingly incompatible forms and images in a single work to express polarities such as vernacular and modern, natural and man-made, free-form and geometric, romantic and rational, which offer a brilliant formal

realization of that vision of an architecture both Modern and Finnish to which his clients asked him to give expression. The modernity of its spatial and formal composition is given a readily-understood national inflection by the references to the vernacular and the evocation of 'forest space', but the building's 'Finnishness' runs deeper than this, for the whole conception can be interpreted as a transformation of the kind of traditional farmhouse which, we may recall, was Aalto's first idea for the design.

Finnish expression

One can adduce both anecdotal and analytical evidence to support this assertion. We will begin with the former: immediately before committing suicide, Aalto's old friend Gustaf Strengell – an architect and distinguished critic – visited the Finnish folk museum on Seurasaari Island to see the celebrated Niemelä farmstead, **49**, and then made the short journey to Munkkiniemi to visit Aalto, where he explained that he had come to see the modern Niemelä farmstead for the last time.[27] The circumstances give added poignancy to Strengell's remark, but this was surely no idle comment, and applies even more readily to the Villa Mairea whose incremental organization around an implied – rather than fully enclosed – courtyard, follows the pattern of Finnish farmsteads.

Strengell's comment might have provided the starting point for a remarkable essay on Finnish vernacular farmhouses by Ranulph Glanville in which he contends that 'the very existence of such courtyards both internal and external, in virtually every Finnish building, is fundamental to the essence of Finnish architecture, from the remotest past right up to the present day'.[28] Glanville suggests that the courtyard form embodies four distinct ideas: firstly, it allows the *completeness* of the form at any stage – the whole can be implied by fragments; secondly, buildings can be extended to fill up the perimeter – there is a principle of *adding on*; thirdly, each function has its *appointed position* within the whole; and fourthly, there is a blurring of conventional distinctions between *inside* and *outside*.

Each of these ideas can be applied directly to the Villa Mairea, and it is tempting to argue even more specifically that the Villa is a contemporary interpretation of the farmsteads which are typical of Pohjanmaa (Ostrobothnia) – an area where the influence of bourgeois Swedish ideas was strongest and especially appropriate therefore for the Swedish-speaking Gullichsens. There, Glanville observes, 'the courtyard is an organisational entity, often inferred with all the subtlety and coolness that Mies used in the Barcelona Pavilion' – or, one might add, that Aalto used in the Villa Mairea.

The additive character of the courtyard is reflected in the vernacular practice of adding on non-integral features to emphasize particular parts of a building such as the entrances or windows – a practice akin to the collage-like composition of the Villa. And lest I be thought to be taking the analogies too far, there is a final, compelling parallel in the internal organization of the main living space. Aalto's essay entitled 'The Dwelling as a Problem', to which we have already referred for evidence of his early commitment to the 'scientific' aspirations of Modernism, begins with observations about the *tupa* (living room) of a peasant farmhouse. It was, Aalto tells us, 'a combination of different functions' and 'was never, before its period of decline, combined with the concept of "room"'. A dwelling, he argues, 'is an area which should offer protected areas for meals, sleep, work, and play'.[29] In the traditional *tupa* these 'protected areas' were defined by means of poles which cross the space just above head height; 'rooms' were implied rather than enclosed, but the location of activities was no less precise because the patterns of use were socially codified. The *tupa* provided the model for Gallen-Kallela's celebrated studio-home, and in the living room of the Villa Mairea Aalto likewise deployed changes of floor level and finish, columns and screens, walls and book-cases, to precisely similar ends – as in his larger buildings and complexes, the Villa is organized by providing an actual or implied 'box' for each function.

Regional paradigm

Architecture has occupied a special place in Finnish culture throughout the 20th century: National Romanticism provided a focus for political dissent, and Modernism – or Functionalism as it is known in Scandinavia – gained ready acceptance in progressive circles as an expression of the social democratic ideals of the newly independent nation-state. Aalto, as we have seen, quickly assimilated the lessons of the new architecture and enriched its abstract language of form and space by manifold allusions to tradition and nature. In place of the general proposition he sought a poetic, highly personal celebration of the particular and a unique sensitivity to the individual psyche; in place of the international he developed a regional manner rooted in national traditions and in the Finnish climate and landscape; in place of the mechanistic he offered a variety and growth reminiscent of natural organic form. Although it is now half a century old, the Villa Mairea retains a remarkable capacity to challenge and inspire the contemporary search for an humane, regionally-inflected and ecologically-responsive Modern architecture.

47

48

49

Photographs

Top left the main entrance is approached up 'rustic' steps beneath a free-form entrance canopy.

Bottom left the timber construction of the sauna is a Japanese-inspired refinement of Finnish vernacular buildings.

Right the outdoor terrace and sauna are enclosed by a low stone wall reminiscent of medieval churchyards.

Left general view from the garden, with the terrace and single-storey dining room on the left and the timber-clad studio on the right.
Right the corner of the house is visually dissolved by the undulating line of poles and climbing plants.

Below view from the covered terrace towards the main living room, with the overtly Japanese screen to the garden room on the right, below the large studio window.
Right the paving and sauna steps and door similarly evoke memories of Japanese tea-houses.

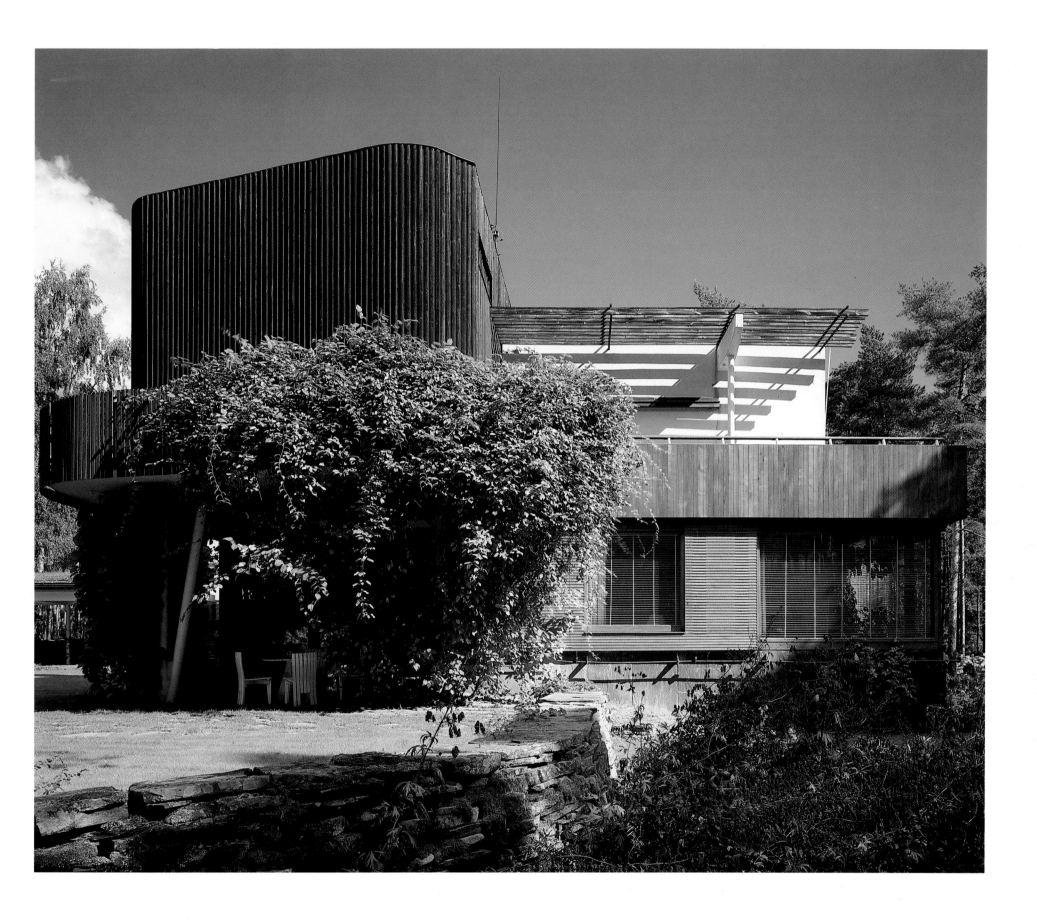

Left corner of the living room, with Maire
Gullichsen's bedroom above and studio
behind.
Above the timber-boarded studio and
balcony wrap around the corner of the
house above the garden room.

Opposite the roof is transformed into a
Japanese dry-garden enclosed by a
curvilinear 'nautical' balustrade.
Above left the corner of the dining room
is a rich collage of materials, colours and
textures.
Right the base of the living room is clad
with granite sheets and the windows have
external teak-slatted blinds.

Left the living room is entered up a
small flight of steps and the eye is
drawn diagonally across to the fireplace.
Above the main staircase is screened
by circular timber poles; the fixing details
recall the growth rings of the bamboo
shown on an early sketch.

Left the corner of the living room is
framed by the library and garden room
and the columns rhyme with the trees
outside.

Above view towards the main staircase
and entrance; the glazed slot above the
library bookcase on the right suggests a
horizontal slice of forest.

Left the white-plastered fireplace recalls vernacular houses.
Above the first tread is articulated to mark the transition between the living room and staircase.

Opposite the winter garden was used by Maire Gullichsen for flower arranging. Note the Katsura Palace-inspired shelves by the window.
Top right interior of Maire Gullichsen's first floor studio.
Bottom right view from the living room towards the winter garden.

Above the main entrance door: the bronze handle recalls the sections of tree-branches used as handles on vernacular buildings.
Right interior of the library which provided a private study and meeting room for Harry Gullichsen.
Far right the door-handles throughout the Villa were purpose-designed by Aalto.

Interior of the kitchen.

Drawings

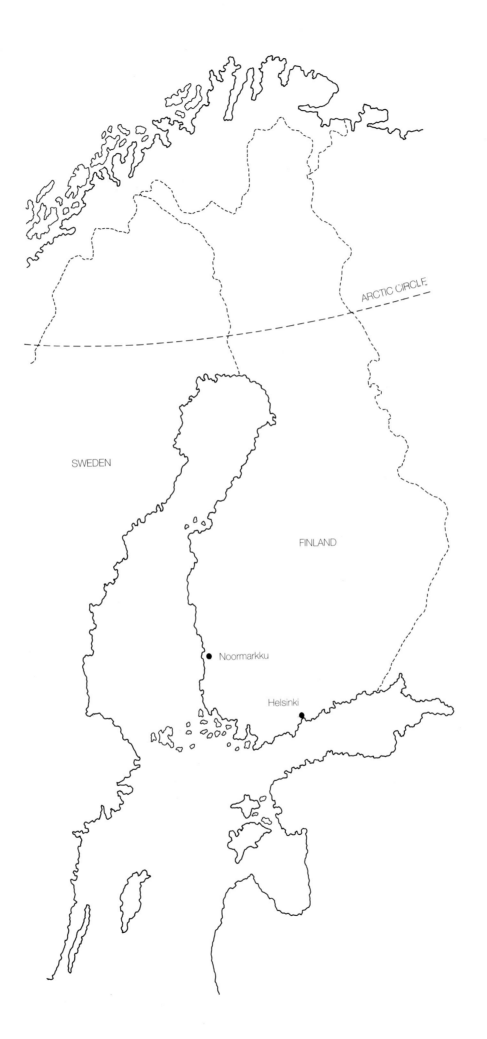

The Villa Mairea was built near to
Noormarkku, a small village located a few
miles inland from the port of Pori on
Finland's west coast.

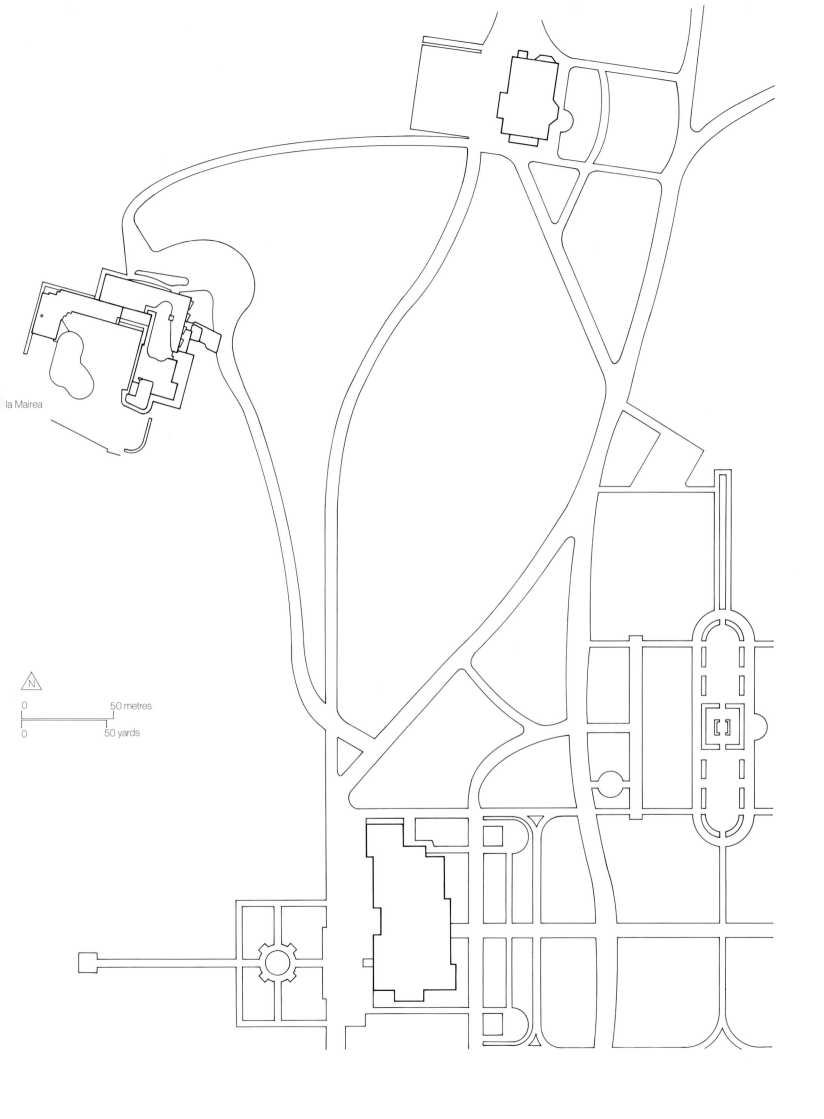

la Mairea

N

| 0 | 50 metres |
| 0 | 50 yards |

Site plan
The Villa Mairea is approached through the entrance court of the art nouveau villa built by Maire Gullichsen's parents. Unlike the earlier houses with their formal gardens, the Villa Mairea is built in a small clearing in the forest.

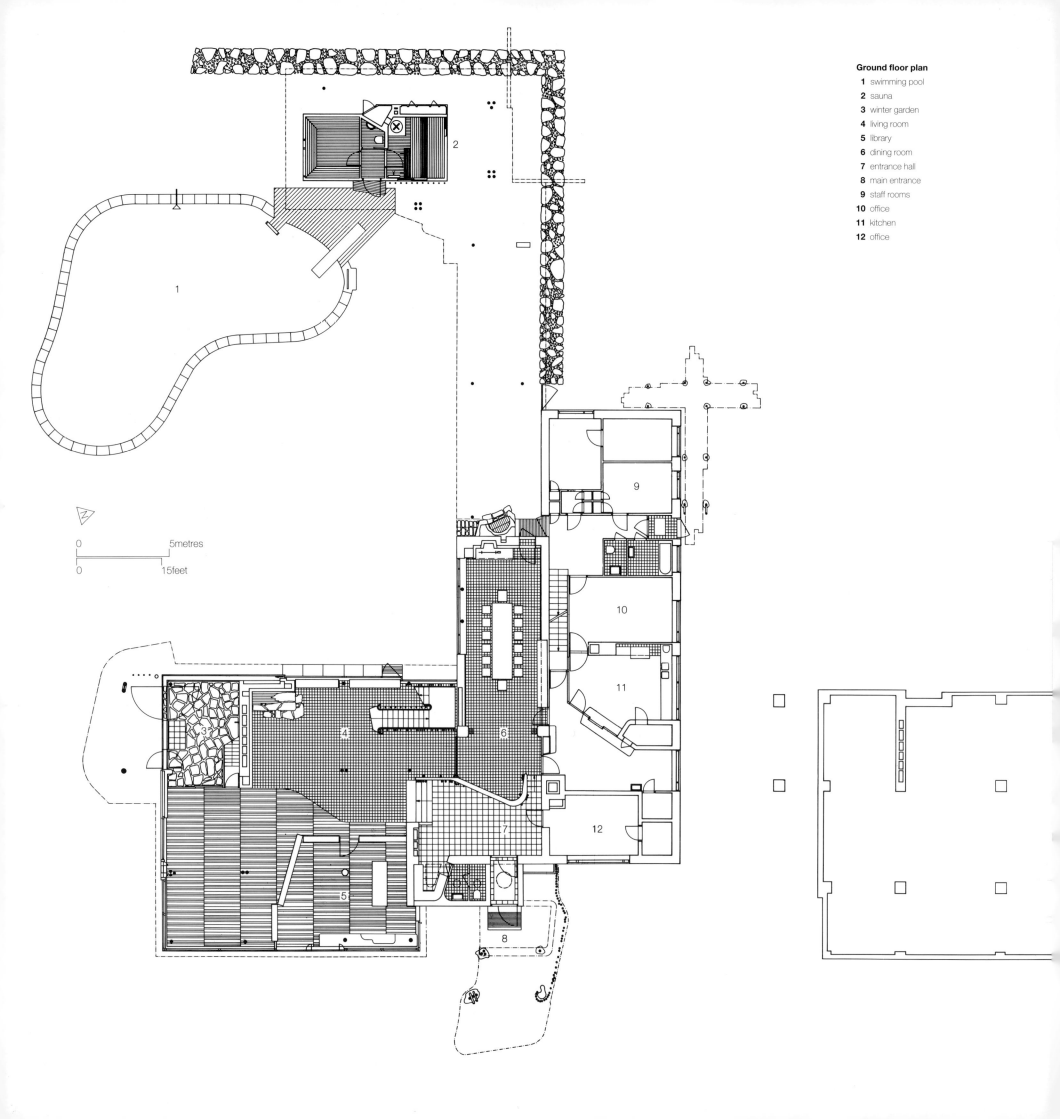

Ground floor plan

1 swimming pool
2 sauna
3 winter garden
4 living room
5 library
6 dining room
7 entrance hall
8 main entrance
9 staff rooms
10 office
11 kitchen
12 office

0   5metres

0   15feet

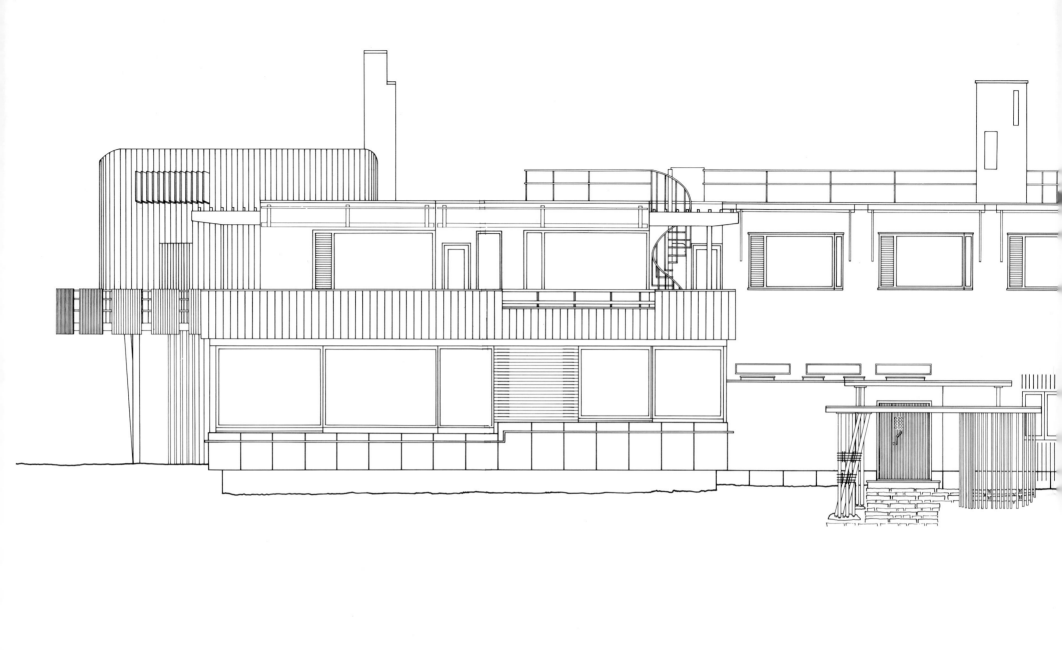
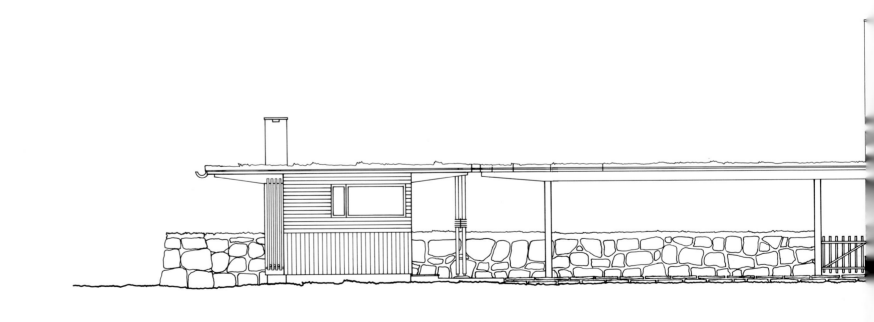

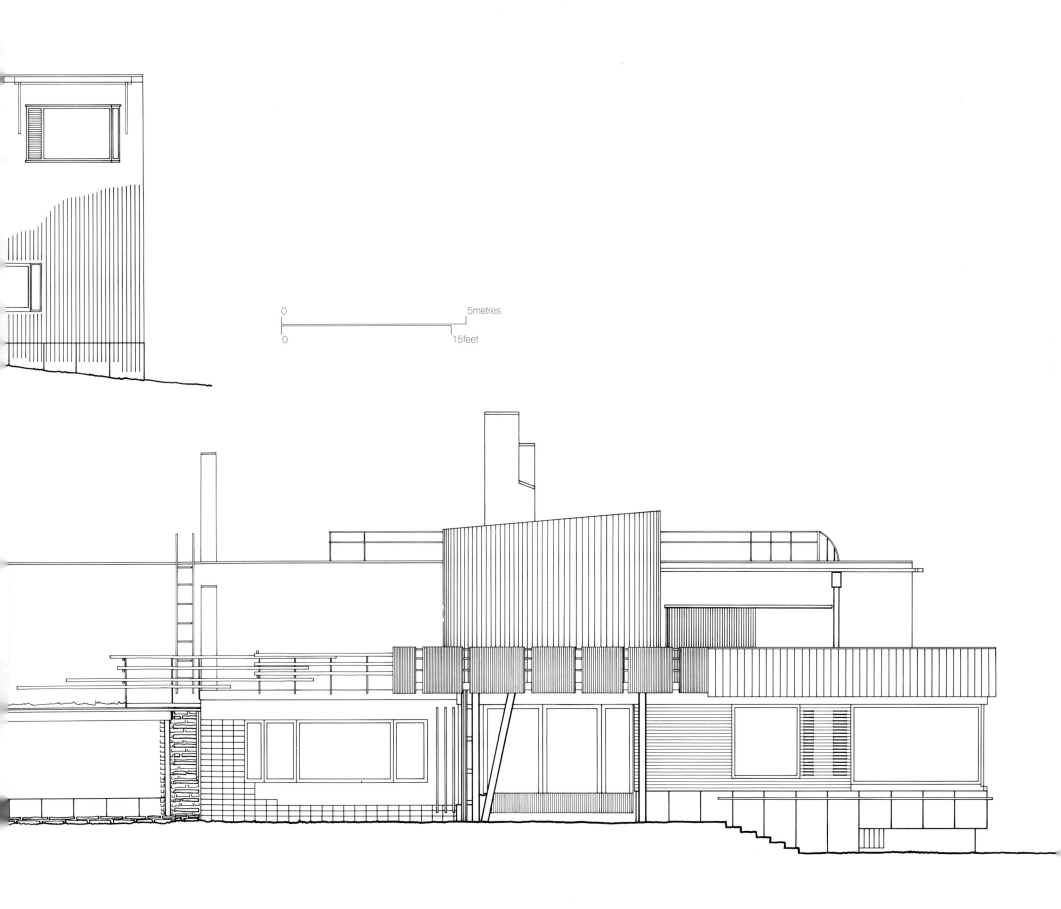

Elevation to the south-east, top;
with elevation to the south-west,
below

0   5metres

0   15feet

Elevation to the north-west, top;
with elevation to the north-east,
below

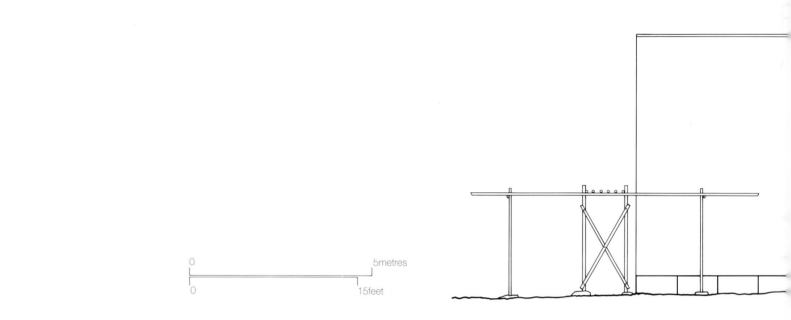

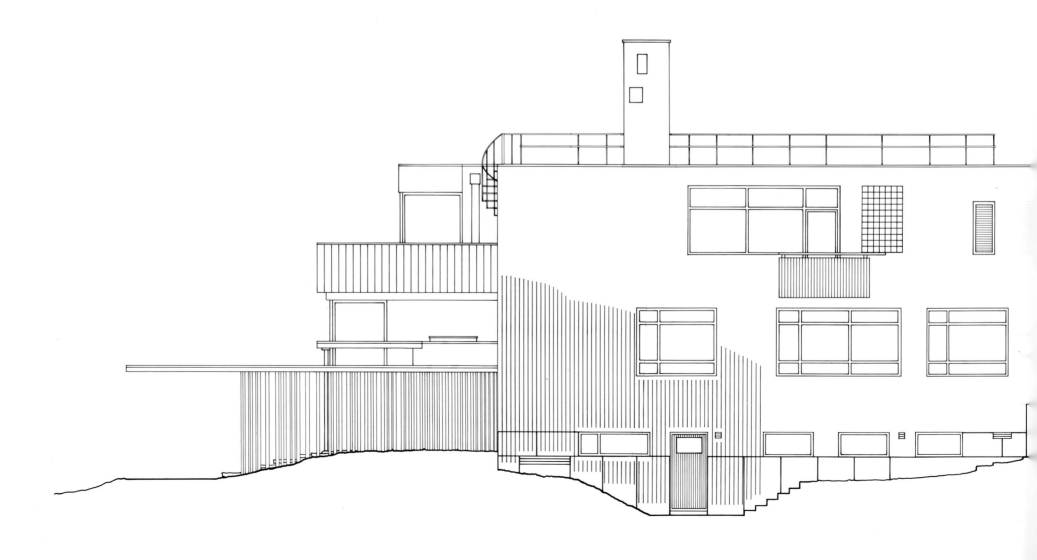

0   5metres

0   15feet

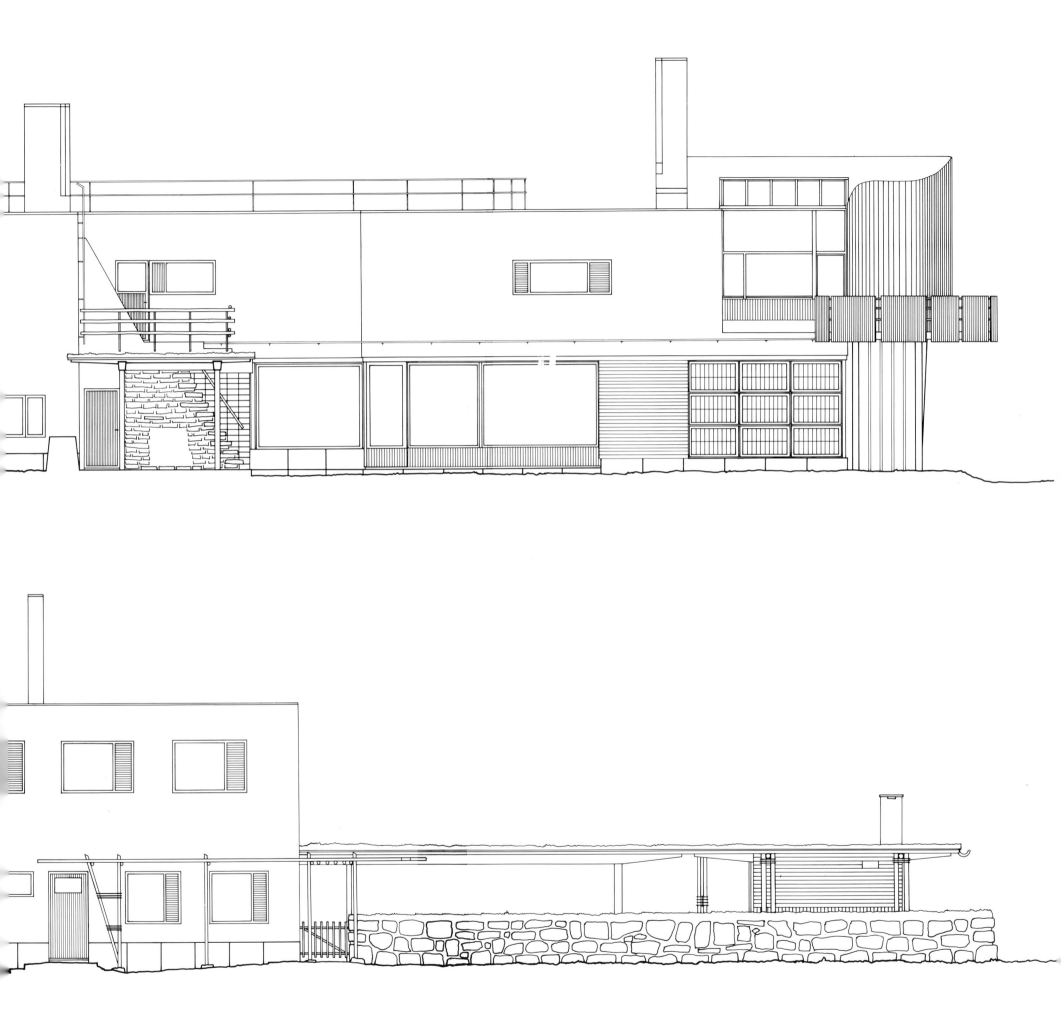

Long section through living room
looking north-west

1 studio
2 winter garden
3 upper hall with fireplace
4 living room
5 children's hall/playroom
6 dining room
7 store
8 kitchen
9 laundry

0   5metres
0   15feet

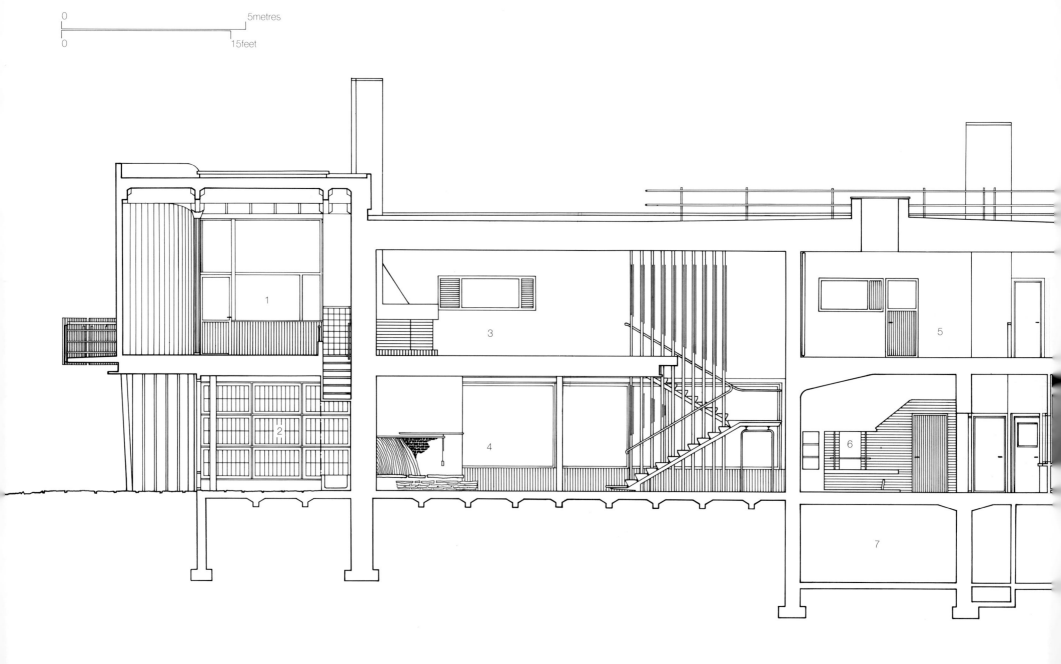

Cross-section through living room
looking south-west

1 studio
2 winter garden
3 master bedroom
4 living room
5 library

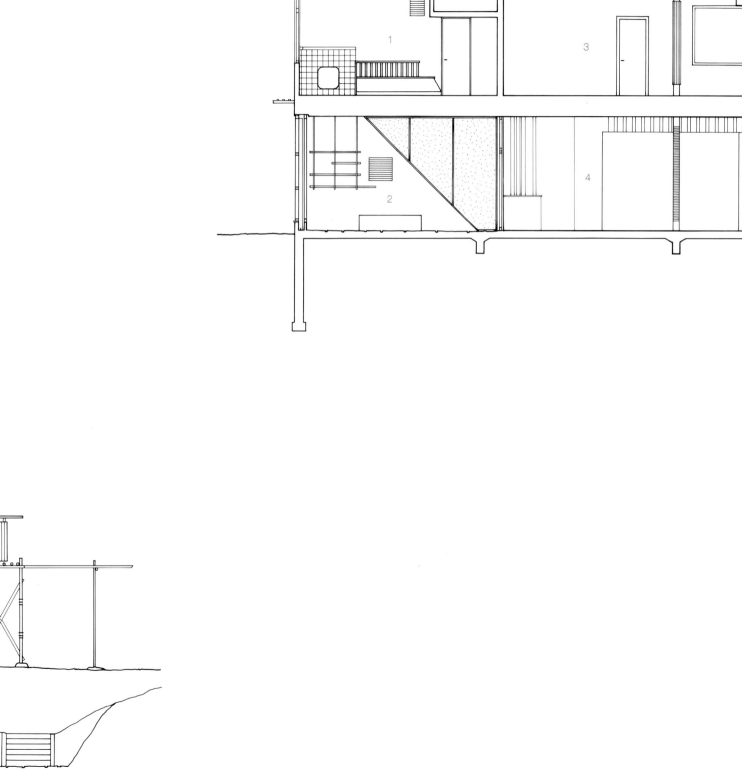

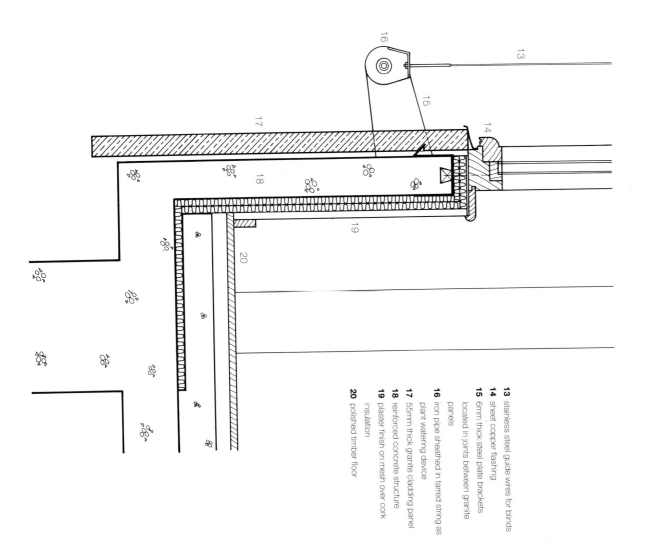

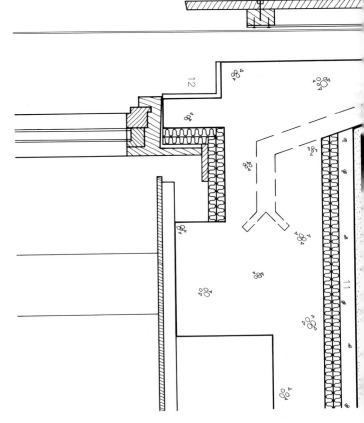

13 stainless steel guide wires for blinds
14 sheet copper flashing
15 6mm thick steel plate brackets
located in joints between granite
panels
16 iron pipe sheathed in tarred string as
plant watering device
17 55mm thick granite cladding panel
18 reinforced concrete structure
19 plaster finish on mesh over cork
insulation
20 polished timber floor

0

200mm

8inches

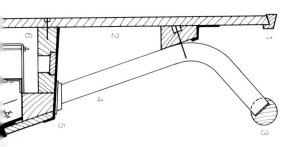

1 teak capping
2 25mm thick teak panel
3 70mm diameter teak handrail
4 50mm diameter tubular steel
   balustrade
5 sheet copper flashing
6 100 x 50mm steel channel framing
7 reinforced concrete structure
8 bituminous waterproof membrane
9 tiles on cement screed
10 teak decking
11 two layers of 25mm thick cork
   insulation
12 cement render finish to soffit

31 cement render finish
32 tiled gutter and upstand
33 tiles on cement screed
34 bituminous waterproof membrane
35 holed brick infill
36 plaster finish on mesh over cork
   insulation

21 sheet copper capping
22 cement render finish
23 blind mechanism bolted to concrete
24 recess for blind
25 cement render finish
26 granite chippings
27 bituminous waterproof membrane
28 concrete screed laid to falls
29 reinforced concrete structure
30 plaster finish on mesh over cork
   insulation

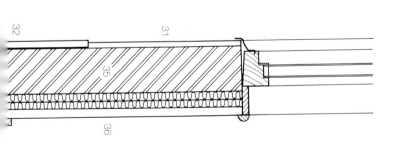

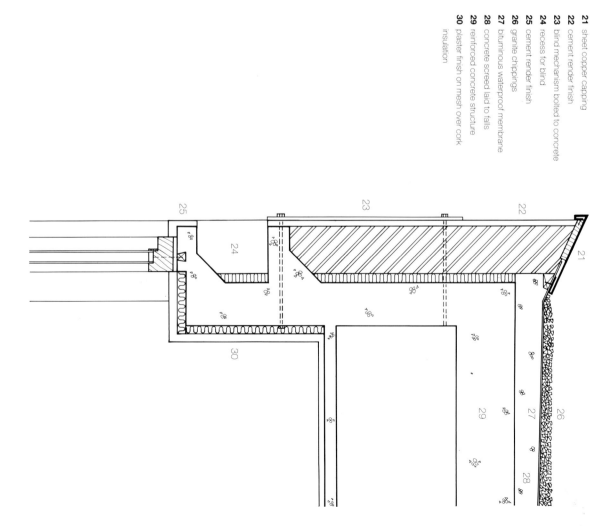

Section through roof terrace above sauna

1 hollowed log gutter held on 25×6mm galvanized steel plate brackets at 500mm centres
2 galvanized steel brackets at 500mm centres
3 birch sapling kerb
4 birch bark mat
5 retaining net
6 turf layer
7 waterproof membrane
8 tongued and grooved decking
9 150 x 25mm planed edge planks
10 100 x 50mm planed edge joists
11 1.5mm thick copper flashing

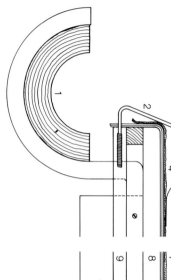
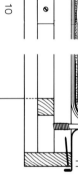

0 100mm
0 4inches

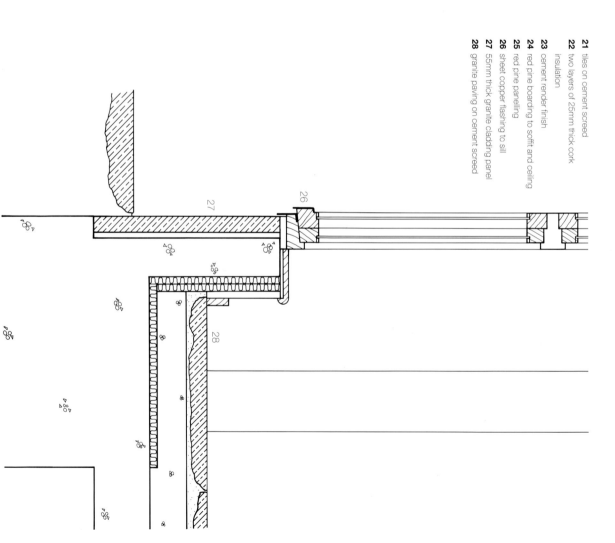

21 tiles on cement screed
22 two layers of 25mm thick cork insulation
23 cement render finish
24 red pine boarding to soffit and ceiling
25 red pine panelling
26 sheet copper flashing to sill
27 55mm thick granite cladding panel
28 granite paving on cement screed

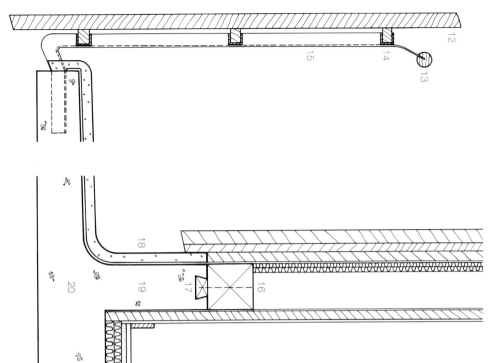

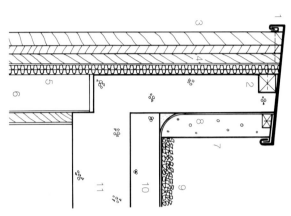

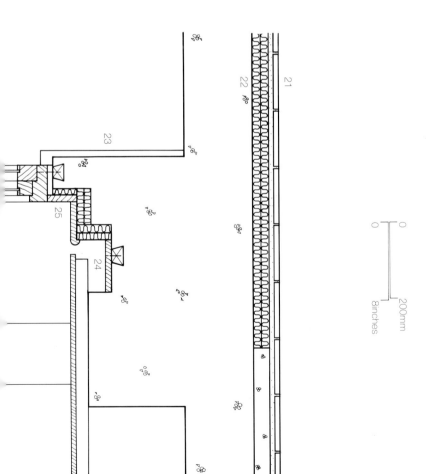

Detailed section through studio and garden room

1 sheet copper capping
2 timber batten let into concrete
3 teak panelling on timber sheathing
4 bituminous waterproof membrane
5 two layers of 25mm thick cork insulation
6 125 × 50mm timber studs at 600mm centres
7 75mm thick concrete sheathing
8 bituminous waterproof membrane
9 granite chippings
10 concrete screed laid to falls
11 reinforced concrete structure

12 red pine boarded balustrade
13 40mm diameter red pine handrail
14 40 × 35mm channel horizontal frame member
15 40 × 60mm channel vertical frame member with flanges cut away at handrail
16 125 × 125mm timber sole plate
17 timber batten let into concrete
18 cement render finish
19 bituminous waterproof membrane
20 reinforced concrete structure

0
0
0
200mm
8 inches

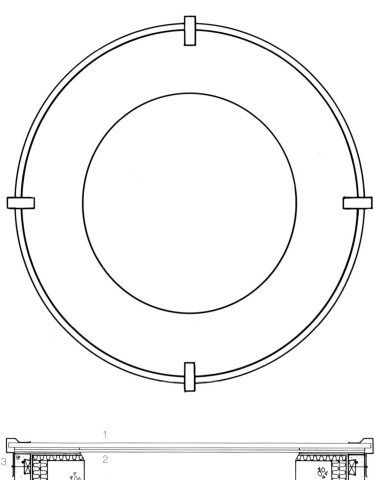

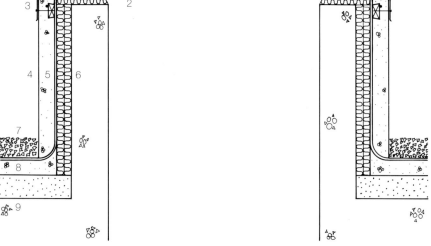

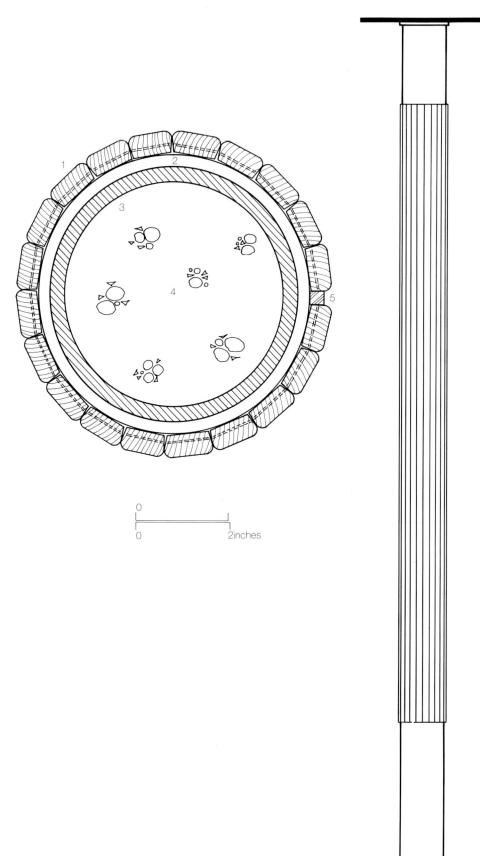

Horizontal section and elevation of beech-clad column

1 12mm thick copper beech cladding secured by brass wire
2 6mm thick asbestos layer
3 135mm diameter CHS column
4 reinforced concrete fill
5 solid brass cover strip

0   200mm

0   8inches

0

0   2inches

Detailed section and plan of 'moon' rooflight

1 12mm thick unpolished diffusing glass
2 6mm thick polished plate glass bedded on bituminous felt
3 25mm wide copper clip fixed to timber strip set into concrete
4 50mm thick sheathing concrete
5 waterproof membrane
6 two layers of 20mm thick cork insulation
7 granite chippings
8 50mm thick concrete above insulation
9 reinforced concrete structure

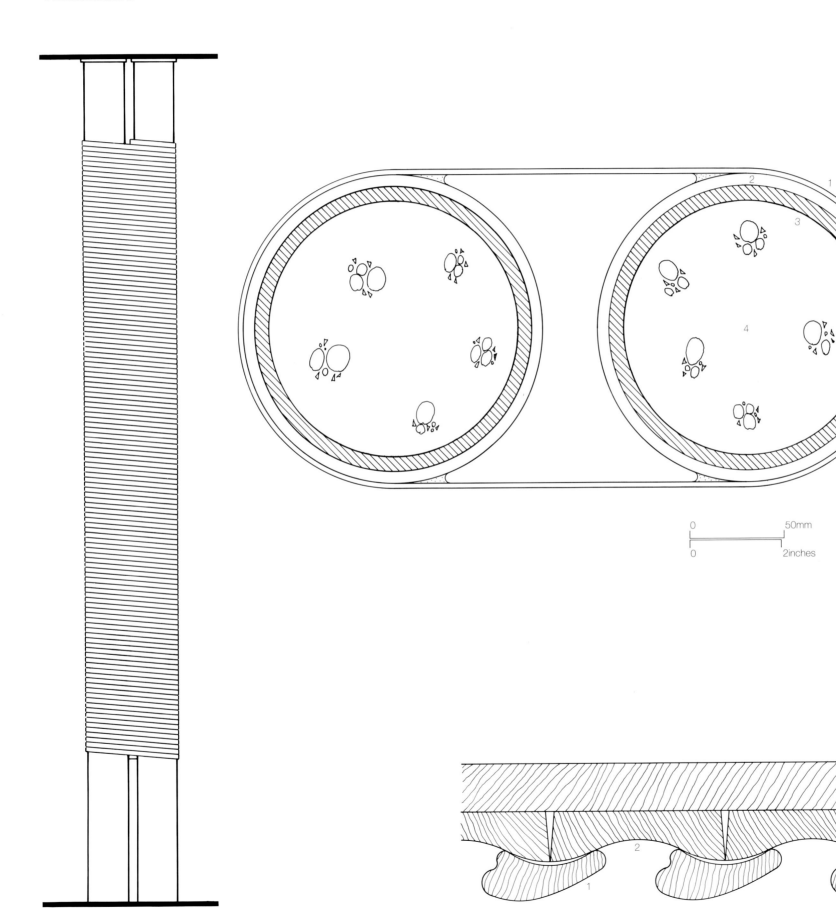

Horizontal section and elevation of twin column

1 rattan sheathing
2 6mm thick asbestos layer
3 150mm diameter CHS column
4 reinforced concrete fill

0   50mm

0   2inches

Horizontal section through red pine panelling in the studio

1 galvanized nailed and plugged profiled batten
2 secret nailed profiled boarding

**Plan and sectional elevations of
main staircase**

A ⌐   ⌐ A

B ⌐   ⌐ B

End elevation

Side elevation

0   1metre

0   3feet

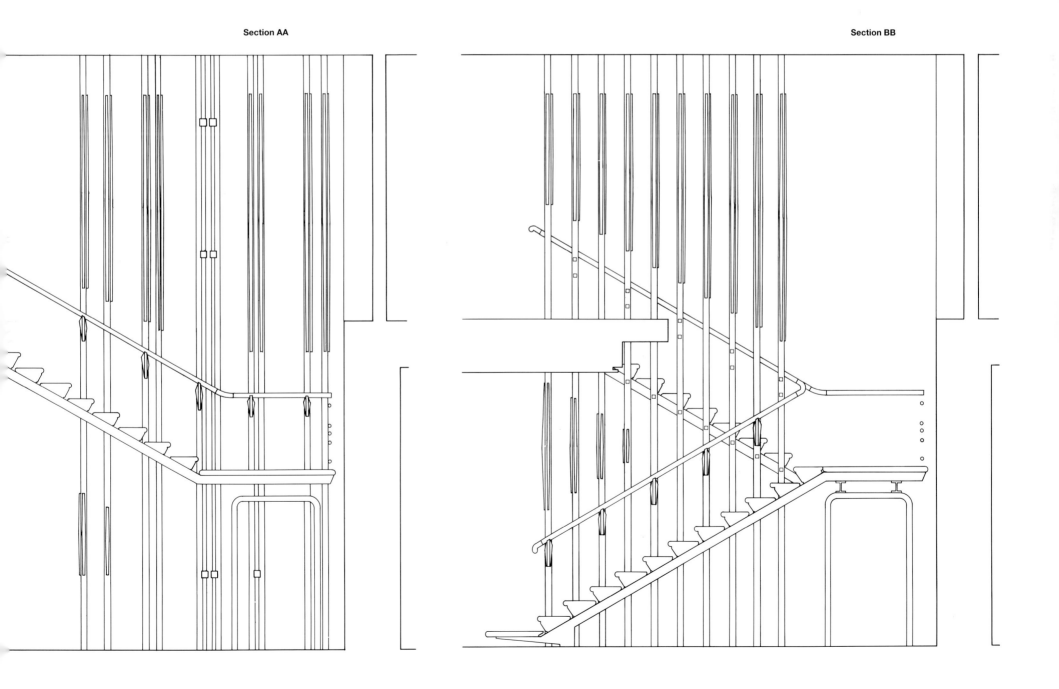

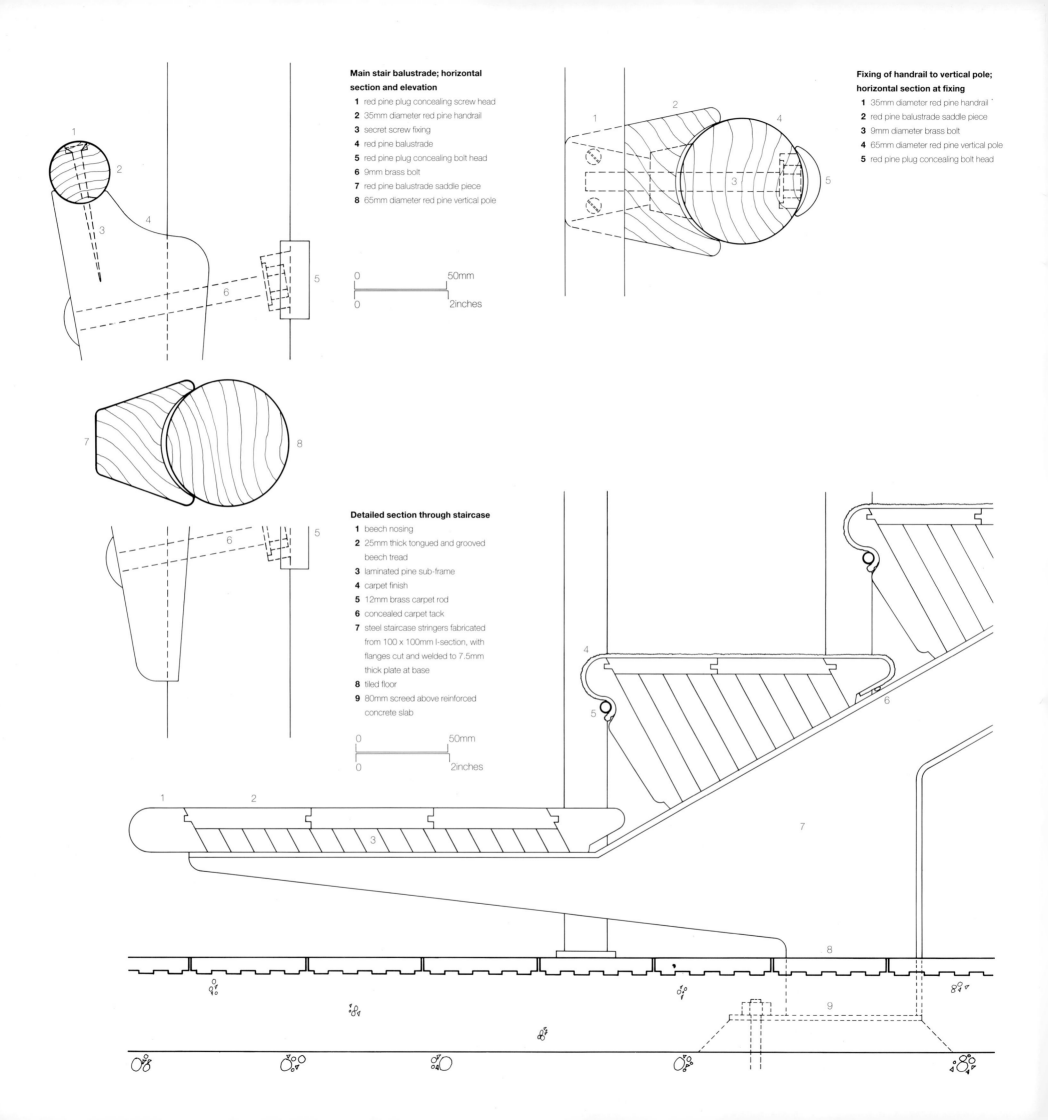

Main stair balustrade; horizontal section and elevation

1 red pine plug concealing screw head
2 35mm diameter red pine handrail
3 secret screw fixing
4 red pine balustrade
5 red pine plug concealing bolt head
6 9mm brass bolt
7 red pine balustrade saddle piece
8 65mm diameter red pine vertical pole

Fixing of handrail to vertical pole; horizontal section at fixing

1 35mm diameter red pine handrail
2 red pine balustrade saddle piece
3 9mm diameter brass bolt
4 65mm diameter red pine vertical pole
5 red pine plug concealing bolt head

0   50mm
0   2inches

Detailed section through staircase

1 beech nosing
2 25mm thick tongued and grooved beech tread
3 laminated pine sub-frame
4 carpet finish
5 12mm brass carpet rod
6 concealed carpet tack
7 steel staircase stringers fabricated from 100 x 100mm I-section, with flanges cut and welded to 7.5mm thick plate at base
8 tiled floor
9 80mm screed above reinforced concrete slab

0   50mm
0   2inches

Main stair balustrade; elevation

1 65mm diameter vertical red pine pole
2 concealed screw fixing
3 35mm diameter red pine handrail
4 9mm diameter brass bolt
5 red pine profiled saddle piece

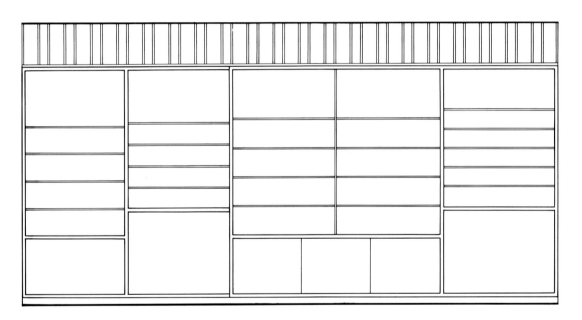

Elevation of the library shelving and screen with horizontal section through serpentine screen

1 red pine beading
2 white papered veneer over 6mm pine board on living room side
3 4mm thick clear glass
4 2mm thick pine veneer on library side

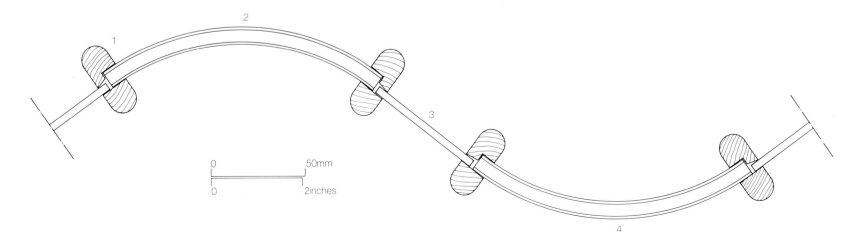

0　　　　　　　　50mm

0　　　　　　　　2inches

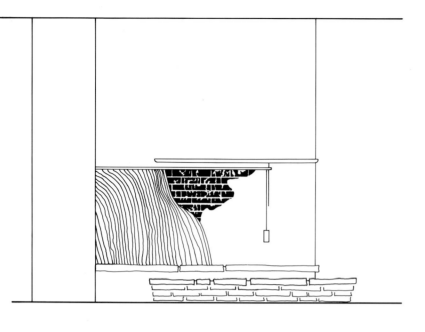

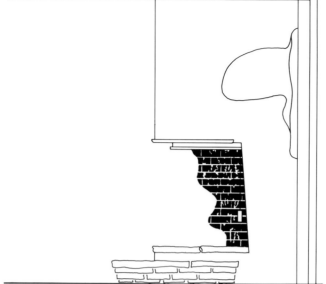

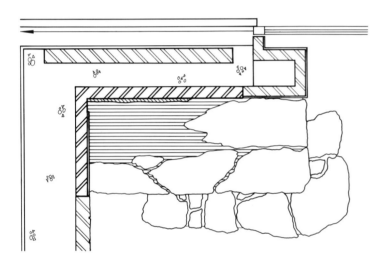

Elevation and plan of fireplace

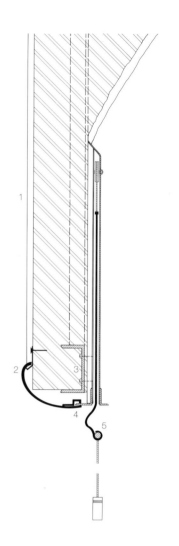

Detailed section through fireplace

1 plaster finish

2 profiled copper nosing

3 100 x 50mm channel lintel

4 35 x 35mm angle supporting 10mm thick fire-proof boarding

5 3mm thick copper sheet sliding fire damper suspended on steel wires and protected by 3mm thick steel sheet

0   100mm

0   4inches

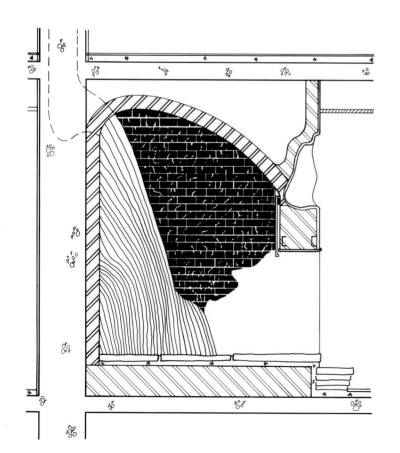

Long section through fireplace

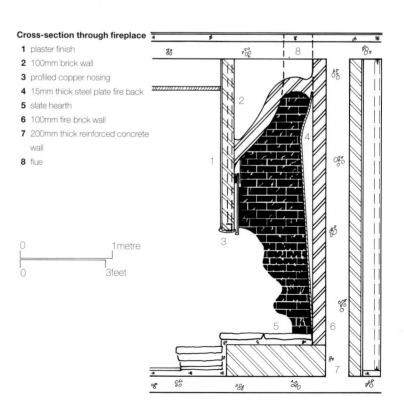

Cross-section through fireplace

1 plaster finish

2 100mm brick wall

3 profiled copper nosing

4 15mm thick steel plate fire back

5 slate hearth

6 100mm fire brick wall

7 200mm thick reinforced concrete wall

8 flue

0   1metre

0   3feet

Select Bibliography

Fleig, K. (ed.) *Alvar Aalto: Band I 1922–1962*, Verlag für Architektur, Artemis, Zürich, 1963.

Pallasmaa, J., 'Villa Mairea – fusion of Utopia and Tradition'. In GA: *Alvar Aalto: Villa Mairea, Noormarkku, Finland, 1937–39* (ed. Y. Futagawa) Tokyo, 1985.

Pearson, P.D., *Alvar Aalto and the International Style*, The Mitchell Publishing Company, New York, 1978.

Porphyrios, D., *The Sources of Modern Eclecticism*, Academy Editions, London, 1982.

Quantrill, M., *Alvar Aalto: a critical study*, Secker and Warburg, London, 1983.

Ruusuvuori, A., *Alvar Aalto 1898-1976*, Museum of Finnish Architecture, Helsinki, 1985.

Schildt, G., *Alvar Aalto: The Early Years*, Rizzoli, New York, 1984.

Schildt, G., *Alvar Aalto: The Decisive Years*, Rizzoli, New York, 1986.

Notes

1 Göran Schildt, *Alvar Aalto: The Decisive Years*, Rizzoli, New York, 1986, p.152. This is the second of Schildt's three-part biography of Aalto.

2 Le Corbusier (trans. F. Etchells), *Towards a New Architecture*, Architectural Press, London, 1970, p.223.

3 See Simo Paavilainen, 'Nordic Classicism in Finland'. In *Nordic Classicism 1910–30*, Museum of Finnish Architecture, Helsinki, 1982, pp.79–104. Nordic Classicism flourished throughout the Nordic countries during the 1920s. Most of its leading practitioners such as Aalto and Erik Bryggman in Finland and Asplund and Sigurd Lewerentz in Sweden made a seemingly effortless transition to Modernism by the end of the decade.

4 Göran Schildt (ed.) *Sketches: Alvar Aalto*, MIT Press, Cambridge, Mass. and London, 1985, pp.29–33.

5 Ibid, p.63.

6 Reprinted as *Alvar Aalto: Villa Mairea*, Alvar Aalto Museum, Jyväskylä, 1981.

7 Quoted in Paul David Pearson, *Alvar Aalto and the International Style*, The Mitchell Publishing Company, New York, 1978, p.168.

8 Göran Schildt, *Alvar Aalto: The Decisive Years*, Rizzoli, New York, 1986, p.154.

9 Ibid, p.12.

10 Demetri Porphyrios, *The Sources of Modern Eclecticism*, Academy Editions, London, 1982, p.36. Porphyrios's analysis of the Villa Mairea is exemplary, and his thesis that Aalto's work opened the floodgates to eclecticism is a provocative counterpoint to generally accepted interpretations.

11 Göran Schildt, *Alvar Aalto: The Decisive Years*, Rizzoli, New York, 1986, p.156.

12 Ibid, p.157.

13 *Alvar Aalto: Villa Mairea*, Alvar Aalto Museum, Jyväskylä, 1981.

14 Ibid.

15 Klaus Herdeg, *The Decorated Diagram*, MIT Press, Cambridge, Mass. and London, 1985, pp.29–35. Herdeg's book contains an excellent analysis of the Villa Mairea from which I have derived several insights.

16 Ibid, p.32.

17 *Alvar Aalto: Villa Mairea*, Alvar Aalto Museum, Jyväskylä, 1981.

18 Göran Schildt, *Alvar Aalto: The Early Years*, Rizzoli, New York, 1984, pp.153, 214–239. Schildt's discussion of Aalto's debt to painting and his interest in anarchist politics provide an essential background to an understanding of his work.

19 Ibid, pp.220–223.

20 See Juhani Pallasmaa, 'Architecture of the forest'. In *The Language of Wood*, Museum of Finnish Architecture, Helsinki, 1987, pp.16–22. This essay offers an excellent short introduction to characteristic features of Finnish architecture.

21 From an interview with Aalto's site architect, Paul Bernoulli, conducted by my colleague, Darren Stewart Capel in August 1991.

22 Göran Schildt, *Alvar Aalto: The Decisive Years*, Rizzoli, New York, 1986, p.107.

23 Juhani Pallasmaa, 'Villa Mairea – fusion of Utopia and Tradition'. In GA: *Alvar Aalto: Villa Mairea, Noormarkku, Finland, 1937–39* (ed. Y. Futagawa) Tokyo, 1985.

24 Kenneth Frampton, *Modern Architecture 1920–45*, Rizzoli, New York, 1983, p.411.

25 From the interview with Darren Stewart Capel.

26 Göran Schildt, *Alvar Aalto: The Decisive Years*, New York, 1986, pp.117–118.

27 Ibid, p.130.

28 Ranulph Glanville, 'Finnish Vernacular Farmhouses'. *Architectural Association Quarterly*, 9(1), 1977, pp.36–51. Glanville's essay is a valuable addition to the modest literature in English on Finnish vernacular buildings, and concludes with a highly speculative comparison of the additive character of much Finnish architecture and the 'agglutinative' structure of the Finnish language.

29 Alvar Aalto, 'The Dwelling as a Problem'. In *Sketches: Alvar Aalto* (ed. Göran Schildt), MIT Press, Cambridge, Mass. and London, 1985, p.29.

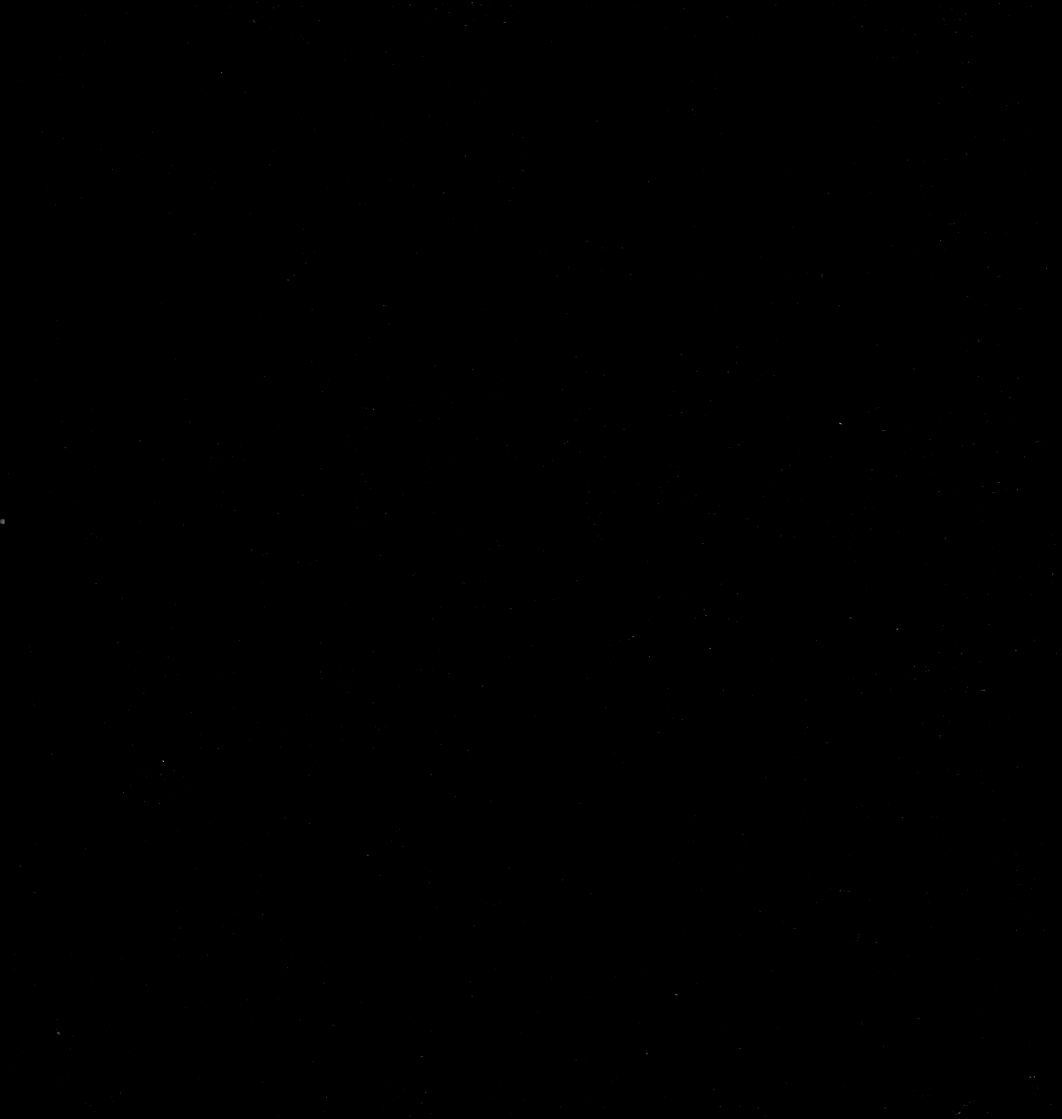

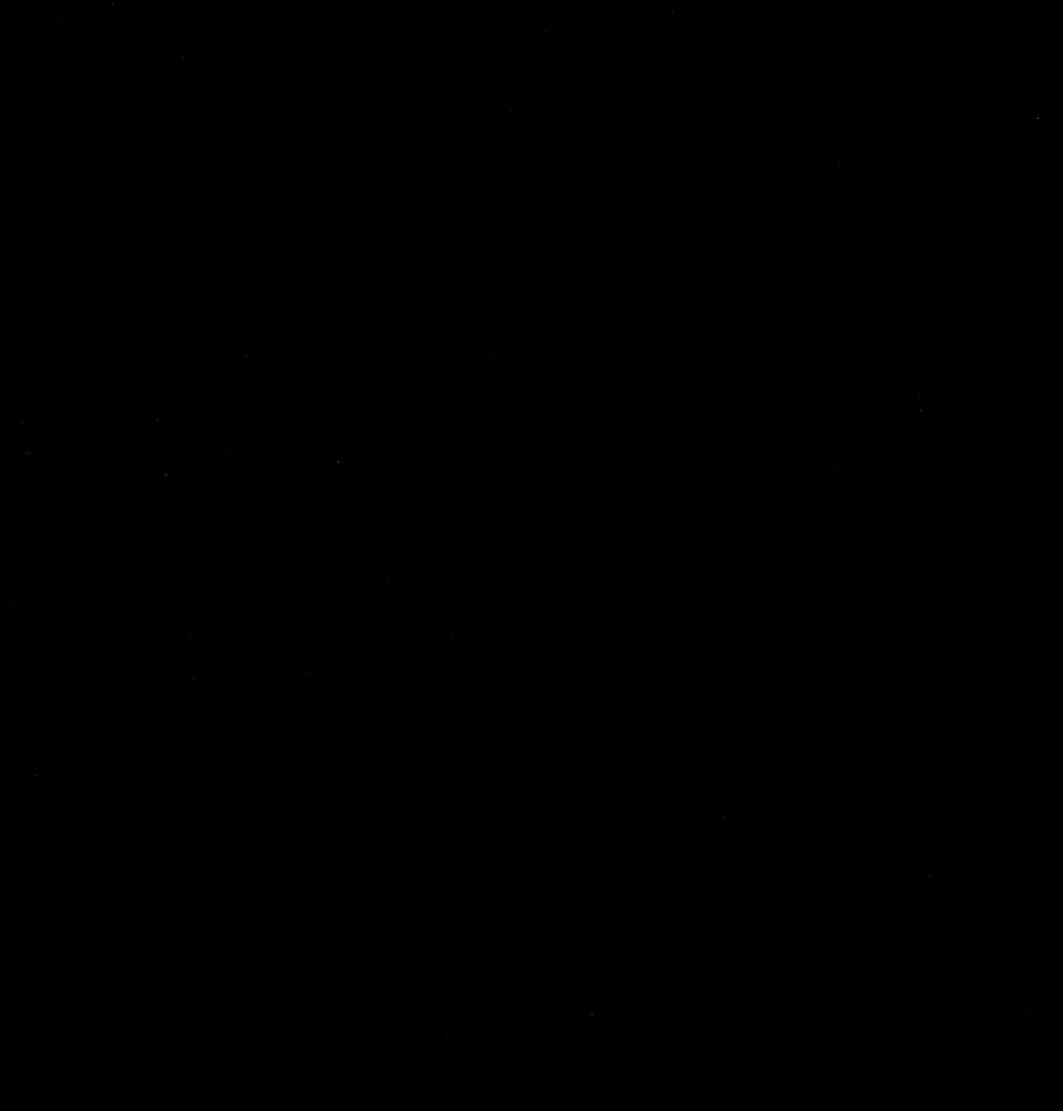

Charles and Ray Eames
Eames House
Pacific Palisades, California 1949

James Steele

Photography
Tim Street-Porter; cover detail
also by Tim Street-Porter
Drawings
John Hewitt

The Eames House, or Case Study #8 as it is officially known, is the singular product of an unusual and fortunate set of circumstances which, in retrospect, seem quite improbable. Like almost everyone else in Los Angeles, Charles and Ray Eames, who designed the house for themselves, came to the city from somewhere else, which in Charles' case was the heartland of the country. Born in St Louis, Missouri on 17 June 1907, he was the son of Marie Lambert and Charles Ormand Eames, and had a textbook, Horatio Alger childhood that included jobs in a printing shop and grocery store, and a dog named Topsy. Eames became interested in photography at the age of 13, and an apocryphal story, perpetuated by his family, relates how he discovered a box of materials necessary for developing by the wet plate process, left behind after the death of his father, an amateur photographer, and was clever enough to discover how it worked, a year before he found out about the existence of film.[1]

Following a part-time job as a labourer in the Laclede steel mill in Venice, Illinois while he was still in high school (which extended to full-time during the summer, to include the construction of concrete forms and patterns as well as minor engineering work), he was offered a scholarship in architecture at Washington University in St Louis.[2] After beginning his studies in 1925, he worked as a draughtsman in the office of Trueblood and Graf, but left the university at the end of his second year. Opening an architectural office for the first time is difficult under the best circumstances, but at the beginning of the Depression, it was virtually impossible. Having designed three houses, Charles and his partners Walter E Pauley and Charles M Gray closed their office in 1934, after a four year struggle. A year later after assisting in the compilation of a Historic American Buildings Survey administered by the Public Works Administration, and a brief trip through San Luis Postosi and Monterrey, Mexico, Charles returned to St Louis, and established a new firm called Eames and Walsh.[3] Their design for St Mary's Catholic Church, in Helena, Arkansas, which was completed in 1936, was the largest commission Eames had yet realized, and proved to be a turning point in his career.

The fundamental Latin cross scheme that he used in the design of St Mary's, as well as his attitude toward simplicity of line and material, and attention to detail were remarkably different from the accumulation of historical references which was so popular at that time;[4] and, when the church was published in *Architectural Forum*, it came to the attention of Eliel Saarinen. Saarinen subsequently wrote a congratulatory letter to Eames; as a result he was offered a fellowship to study architecture at the Cranbrook Academy of Art, in Cranbrook, Michigan, which he accepted in the autumn of 1938, entering with a

2

3

1 Charles Eames, with his sister Adele, at the family home in St Louis, Missouri.
2 As a labourer in the Laclede Steel Company, Charles became involved in the design and construction of formwork, which was invaluable experience for him.
3 Ray Kaiser in 1940, shortly before marriage to Charles in June 1941.
4 While ostensibly contemplating something dire, Charles has knotted a rope at one foot intervals to judge the scale of an exhibition he is planning.

1

class that included Edmund Bacon, Harry Weese, Harry Bertoia and Ralph Rapson.[5] By 1940, his rapid progress enabled him to become head of the Department of Industrial Design at Cranbrook, while also working part-time in the Saarinen office. This was an important year for him in another respect, since it also marked his first visit to California, with Frances Rich, whose mother, the film star Irene Rich, asked him to design a studio for her in Hollywood. While the project never materialized, the experience made him aware of the possibilities available in Los Angeles, and directed his attention toward the city.

In 1940, Eames entered the 'Organic Design in Home Furnishings' competition, organized by the Museum of Modern Art in New York City, along with Eero Saarinen, with whom he had collaborated earlier on an exhibition of faculty work. A condition of the competition, which included Alvar Aalto and Marcel Breuer on its illustrious jury, was that the winners would allow their design to be manufactured and offered for sale at Bloomingdales Department Store, who were sponsoring the effort.[6] The Eames–Saarinen entries, which included various kinds of living-room seating and several tables, caused a sensation due to their incorporation of two new techniques of assembly. Their designs, which were based on the moulding of wood into compound curves, and the cycle welding of rubber to wood, which were then being tested by one of

America's leading automobile manufacturers, were so innovative, and came so close to the intent of the competition brief, that they won easily. The production of the series was thwarted by the war effort, yet the techniques involved formed the basis of Charles Eames' furniture design throughout the following decade. The 'Organic Design' competition was also significant on a more personal level, since Ray Kaiser, who helped prepare drawings and models for the submission, became his wife on 20 June 1941. Born in Sacramento, California, Ray had attended high school and junior college there before going on to the May Friend Bennett School in Mill-brook, New York, and painting studies with Hans Hoffmann in New York City, finally entering Cranbrook in September 1940. Her familiarity with California, combined with the interest generated by Charles' trip there, were instrumental in their decision to move to Los Angeles in July 1941.

The Case Study House programme
The Eameses' friendship with John Entenza, editor of *California Arts & Architecture* magazine, seems to have been established soon after their arrival in Los Angeles, since he helped them find their first apartment there, in the Strathmore Avenue Building in Westwood, designed by Richard Neutra.[7] Soon afterwards, Charles began working on film sets at the Metro Goldwyn Mayer studios in Culver City,

5

6

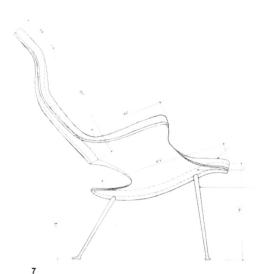

7

5 Charles Eames and John Entenza were close friends as well as collaborators; and Entenza was primarily responsible for the Eameses' quick assimilation into their adopted city.
6 Beginning with rather primitive wooden moulds set up in their first Los Angeles apartment, the Eameses were able to develop complex curves in new industrial materials.
7 Furniture designs, 1940, as conceived by the Eames Studio, involved

8

documentation as precise as that used in building construction.
8 The new layout of Case Study #8, swung around 180° into the embankment from which it once projected, with a courtyard separating the house's living and working components.
9 Charles Eames had many, varied interests, not easily categorized under the general heading of Architecture, which makes an assessment of his work more complex.

9

while he and Ray were also conducting experiments with moulded plywood in a spare room they had converted into a studio. These continued the line of inquiry first begun in the 'Organic Design' submission concerning the formation of three-dimensional, compound curves in a single-moulded operation that could serve as a prototype for assembly-line production, without the need for additional upholstery.[8] These experiments unexpectedly led to a government contract for the design of a formed plywood splint that could be strapped up quickly on the battlefield, and this enabled the Eameses to move into a separate studio off Santa Monica Boulevard in 1942 and to open a factory at 555 Rose Avenue, where Charles converted a loft space into an architectural office.

During this busy time, John Entenza continued to improve his magazine, shortening its name to *Arts & Architecture*, and streamlining the design.[9] The Eameses became more involved with the magazine, Charles becoming an editorial associate and Ray designing many of the covers. In 1943, Entenza organized a competition entitled 'Designs for Postwar Living', and dedicated an entire issue to the results in 1944.[10] This was to prove to be a crucial link to the Case Study programme which followed. As Marilyn and John Neuhart, and Ray Eames have described it, the issue 'was devoted to the prefabrication, mass production and industrialization of residential construction' and contained 'an article by Charles and Entenza entitled "what is a house?"'. Responding to a projected housing shortage in the postwar period, the authors explored the possibilities of using industrial technologies originally developed to meet war-time needs. 'The article,' they continued, 'advocated approaching the impending shortage with the same urgency and energy that was employed in meeting war-time challenges. It reflected the general optimism of planners and designers that the postwar world would bring with it qualitative changes in the way people live and think about their environment and inspire a willingness to make innovative uses of the new technologies developed in wartime.'[11]

The initiative represented in this issue was expanded in January 1945 into an ambitious programme of Case Study houses, intended to implement industrialization, and promote the ideals of Modernism. Initially John Entenza selected eight architects, or firms, who were given a mandate to identify and express the salient characteristics of a new life-style that was seen to be desired by postwar families in southern California. In alphabetical order, the architects chosen were: Thornton Abell, J R Davidson, Charles Eames and Eero Saarinen, Richard Neutra, Ralph Rapson, Whitney Smith, Spaulding and Rex and Wurster and Bernardi. Eventually, this programme was expanded to include 34

10

houses, of which 23 were completed before it ceased when Entenza sold the magazine in 1966.

Details of the first eight houses, along with one for Entenza himself, which became Case Study #9, were presented rapidly in *Arts & Architecture*, following the announcement of the programme.[12] The Eames House, Case Study #8, was designed for a three-acre parcel in Pacific Palisades at the top of a 150 foot high cliff, overlooking the Pacific, a view which it was to share with Case Study #9; an additional two acres was set aside for houses by Richard Neutra and Rodney Walker. Entenza had purchased the entire five acres on behalf of the magazine, from the Will Rogers estate in Santa Monica canyon.[13]

The first design for Case Study #8, by Charles and Ray Eames and Eero Saarinen, with structural consultation by Edgardo Contini, was divided into two volumes of residence and studios, arranged in an 'L', with the living component placed perpendicular to a steep embankment on the northeast side of the site. This allowed it to take full advantage of the view over the Pacific, without intruding on the privacy of the Entenza House nearby. To deal with a substantial slope from the foot of the embankment to the middle of the meadow, which the Eameses and Entenza were to share, Contini had proposed a bridge structure utilizing parallel trusses, partially cantilevered on two slender columns that allowed it to project out over the meadow and an entry drive-

way that passed underneath it. In contrast to this thin linear 'Bridge House', as the Eameses referred to it, the Entenza House, which was treated as its complement, was confined to a single volume, almost square in plan, with a pinwheel framing arrangement that radiates outwards from a central core. The houses were ingeniously sited to retain the integrity of each, while also creating a semi-enclosed green space between them which gradually opened up into the meadow beyond. In their own description of their design intent for both Case Study houses #8 and #9, in their debut in *Arts & Architecture* in December 1945, the architects provide some clues into the agenda of the Case Study programme as well as their own place in it, by saying that they are 'determinedly agreed on the necessity of privacy' and that the houses may both be 'considered as solutions of typical living problems; through meeting specific and rather special needs [where] some contribution to the need of the typical might be developed'.[14] Through frequent references to the need for the house to accommodate 'work and play' and act as a 'background for a life in work', as well as for 'relaxation with friend and foe', the Eameses reiterate their belief in their work ethic that may be seen to be a pattern in both their lives up to this point, and their wish to continue that habit by also using their new house as a design laboratory, just as the Strathmore Avenue apartment had been.[15]

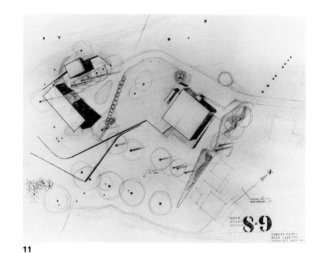

11

10 Following a visit to an exhibition of Mies van der Rohe's work, where Charles had seen a scheme similar to that of his own 'Bridge House', the concept of the Eames House was radically changed, using the same amount of steel, which had already been fabricated.
11 The original site plan of both the rectilinear Eames and square Entenza houses, in which the 'Bridge House' is shown perpendicular to the embankment.

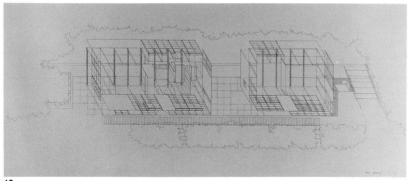

12

13

12 In the new configuration, the house runs parallel to, rather than across a central meadow, giving diagonal views to the Pacific Ocean.

13 Conceived in collaboration with Edgardo Contini, the 'Bridge House', which was separated from the land, directly contradicts the finally realized design.

14 The wall section of the house is remarkable for its spareness, related to a structural rather than visual determination of stability.

15 The final zoning of the

house is based on a flipped plan, in which service areas for living and working components line the central court allowing two storey high open spaces to face outwards.

16 The position and size of wall openings was calculated to allow light and view at certain times of day.

17 Reflections on glass walls were given equal importance to interior shadows, since exterior spaces were considered equal to those in the interior.

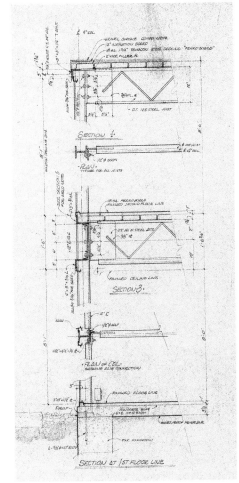

14

16

17

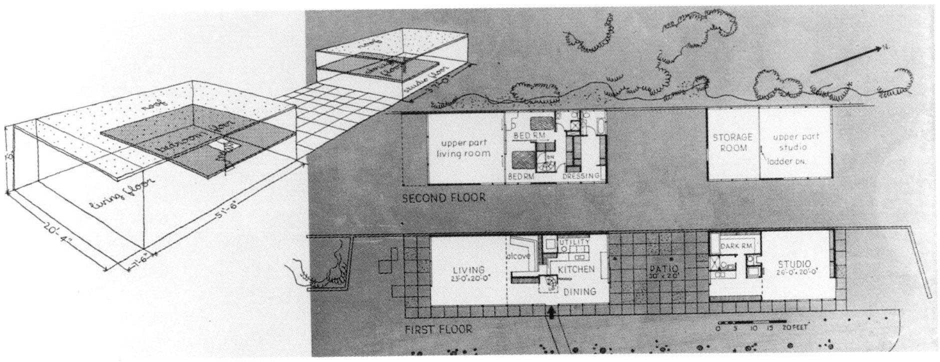

15

In the interim, while the first houses in the Case Study programme (which were all built in wood), were being completed and prepared for the public tours considered to be an essential, didactic part of the entire exercise, Charles Eames attended an exhibition of the work of Mies van der Rohe at the Museum of Modern Art in New York City. He was already very familiar with the architect's work, having travelled to Europe in 1929 specifically to see it, along with buildings by Le Corbusier, Walter Gropius and Henry Van de Velde.[16] References to the effect that the Mies van der Rohe exhibition had on Eames, in the few reminiscences that mention it, are vague, but consistently infer that he returned to Los Angeles determined to alter the 'Bridge House' scheme. In Ray Eames' own account for example, written with John and Marilyn Neuhart, she says: 'the final plan and constructed buildings are quite different from the original conception. After the materials for constructing the house were delivered to the site, Charles changed his mind (influenced perhaps by his visit in November 1947 to an exhibition of the work of Mies van der Rohe at the Museum of Modern Art) about the siting of buildings and worked on a new plan that used the same amount of steel but enclosed more space'.[17] The similarities between the original 'Bridge' scheme and one of the sketches in the exhibition indicate that Charles was concerned about being derivative, and changed the design to avoid this criticism.

The second and final scheme

The new configuration of Case Study House #8, which appeared in the May 1949 issue of *Arts & Architecture*, still takes several cues from Mies van der Rohe, but is much more original in its massing and proportion, as well as in the treatment of all exterior elevations. By pulling the rectilinear living component of the house, which had formed a bridge over the meadow, back in line with the studio along the base of the northeast embankment, the Eameses were able to simplify the scheme considerably; but a retaining wall, which had only been partially necessary before, as part of the studio, was now extended along the hill, becoming a critical, vertical support along that entire side of the house at ground floor level. The second important consequence of this change in orientation, in addition to literally fusing half the house to the land, is that the major sight lines, from the interior, had been redirected toward the Entenza house, with only a diagonal, rather than straightforward view to the sea. To offset this, all of the fill from the excavation for the retaining wall was placed between the two houses, to form an elongated mound, which was then planted as a screen.

Eucalyptus trees were also planted along the open, extended elevations of both the house and studio as a secondary veil, for privacy and shade. These, as well as the vegetation on the cylindrical, artificial mound, provide dense cover; the eucalyptus trees have now become an integral part of the front elevation of the house, to the extent that it is almost completely obliterated by them. The sleek, flat surfaces of the first 'Bridge House' have been changed into a cubic semaphore of light in the accumulated bays, measuring 7ft 6in wide, 20ft long and 17ft high. The 'living' portion of the house has eight bays, with one additional bay used as a shaded overhang. The central court has four, and the studio five. The steel frame that Eames has used is intentionally and remarkably thin, including 4in H-columns for the walls, and 12in deep, open web joists for the roof, with exposed, corrugated metal decking used as a ceiling.[18]

More than any of the Case Study houses built prior to it, the Eames House fulfils the intention of the programme in that it uses prefabricated, standardized parts, and industrial, rather than telluric materials, such as concrete, glass, steel, insulation board on plywood, asbestos and 'pylon', which is not Egyptian, as the brand name would suggest, but a translucent laminate similar to fibreglass. Rather than denying the surroundings of the house, Eames saw these inorganic materials as being complementary to them, because, as he said, 'the texture of the ceiling, the metal joists, the repetition of the standard sash, the change of glazing from transparent to translucent … all add to the architectural relationship of house to nature'.[19] Given the stark contrast

involved, this relationship is obviously not established through a sympathetic use of materials, but through the subtle interaction best expressed in an Eames film called 'House After Five Years of Living'. The film, which has a musical score but no narration, is a paean to the interaction between nature and the house, which, when shown at all, is presented as a means of refracting the natural world around it, or as a lens through which it is to be viewed. A great deal of footage is given to minuscule detail: of the patterns of colour; of leaves on a pathway in front of the house; the shifting dapples of shade cast by the long, narrow, Schindleresque window frames on interior walls; distant views through the trees to the sea; and the changing of the seasons. It is significant that 'House After Five Years of Living', which is ten minutes and four seconds long, is non-sequential and not the result of the continuous panning of a movie-camera through various spaces, but is created out of still images shot by Charles Eames between 1949 and 1955.[20] While seamless, sequential footage could have been easily accomplished, the measured quality of the film is indicative of an attitude toward segments and isolated images, which has carried over into the house itself. The solid panels on the exterior, for example, which are painted in various primary colours that correspond to the character of the functions taking place behind them, like rear-projection movie screens, contribute

18

19

18 Prefabricated steel sections allowed the main frame of the house to be erected in a single day; but finishing took longer.
19 Light gauge steel joists made rapid construction possible.
20 Great care was taken in the placement of solid and glazed panels.
21 An overhang, on the end wall of the living space, cuts down the glare of late afternoon sun.
22 Shadows, constantly moving across walls and floor, are a constant reminder that each room is indeed derivative of the Italian word 'camera'.

20

21

22

23 The concrete retaining wall, making a connection to the hillside possible, is not now as evident as it was in early construction photographs.

24 The steel frame of the house looks especially fragile, almost ephemeral, before enclosure.

25 The simple expedient of a balcony makes the spaces register as being more complex and lofty.

26 Seen from above, the living area appears to be cavernous, in spite of its relatively modest height, due to the judicious positioning of openings.

27 The line of eucalyptus trees planted for privacy, has now become integrally related to the major elevation of the house.

28 Curtains on the end wall of the living space also reduce heat gain, and an outside patio there was a favourite place to enjoy late afternoon sun.

23

24

25

26

27

28

to this impression of refraction by selectively framing views through the transparent glass around them, just as pre-arranged garden vignettes are framed in the classic Japanese house.

In plan, the various parts are also arranged to provide similar kinds of experiences, in staccato sequence. A pathway, beginning at the drive, leads up to the main entrance into the residential component of the two separate columns, which is directly opposite a spiral stair. This is the only means of access to the first floor, and is made of steel beams cut into flanges, welded onto a central pipe column, with stair treads of thin plywood providing another reminder of Eames' affection for this material. A dining, kitchen and utility area, to the right of the main entrance, face onto the central court, echoing the service core of mechanical spaces and a dark-room that does the same, in the studio directly opposite.[21] By grouping the services in both the house and the studio at the court's edge in this way, a contrapuntal, positive and negative rhythm of spaces is set up, connected by narrow passages. These major volumes are the studio, which is double height, with a balcony overlooking the studio from the dark-room core, and the central court, which was originally intended to have a steel arcade on its one open edge. This is now enclosed on three sides only, and is open to the meadow and the living room of the house, which also has an overlooking balcony from the bedroom above. The positioning of the windows on the uphill gradient, in both the house and studio walls that rest on concrete, are far from arbitrary, and help to amplify this metronomic approach to closed and open space. Solid, windowless walls are used where there are double-height spaces, and windows appear at both the upper level office in the studio and the bedroom on the first floor of the house. This language of fenestration, in which the windows appear to be used like apertures, carefully positioned in either conjunction or opposition to others on each side of both major volumes, is a singular attribute that slowly reveals itself, and is easily overlooked in the visual excitement caused by the materials that are used. It was this kind of interplay, caused by control over natural light through the fine-tuning of openings that are juxtaposed and calibrated with the mechanical precision of an F-stop, that Eames was trying to convey in the film 'House After Five Years of Living'. Here he was able to realize fully the registration of the diurnal cycle as the sun moved in its daily diagonal line across the house.[22] The importance of this degree of control over the extent to which nature, manifested as light and air and view, is allowed to penetrate into the various interior spaces, was obviously very important to Charles and Ray Eames, and while only hinted at in their writings, it is clear in their film where great attention is paid to light and shadow.

As they also indicated in this description, their house is a highly personalized expression of their particular style, as it developed shortly after their move to California, and remained throughout their married life. Having met through work on the 'Organic Design in Home Furnishings' competition, that aspect of their relationship remained a key part of their residence. This is confirmed by Charles' description (his equivalent of Le Corbusier's statement that a house 'is a machine for living'), that it is 'a centre for productive activity'.[23] The studio was the focal point of that activity in the beginning of the Eameses stay in Pacific Palisades, until the size of the space was no longer adequate to handle the projects they were involved in. The studio served as their home office until 1958, when the Herman Miller Furniture Company moved out of their quarters at 910 Washington Boulevard in Venice, California, and it became the new Eames office.

'House After Five Years of Living', which is the most accurate document of the interiors as they were when the Eameses lived there, also shows the extensive attention lavished on the various collections that began to accumulate, reinforcing the impression of their fondness for categorizing and miniaturization. Rather than replicating the positivist gestalt implied by the pioneers of Modernism, volume is treated as a neutral background for images, which are either reflected, or composed. Space is not treated as a tangible substance to be contained, or as some mystical, ameliorative substance that would gradually uplift and transform those who experience it, but as the logical consequence of structure. The infectious, child-like delight taken in details may also be seen in other films, such as 'Toy Trains' and 'Tops' which elevate adolescent playthings to fine art; as does their Revell Toy House, intended by the Herman Miller Furniture Company to be a room-planning guide, complete with ¾in scale Eames furniture and accessories.[24] The Eames House is the apotheosis of this relative, microscopic attention to detail, the architectural embodiment of the office's most famous film, 'Powers of Ten', which, by examining the similarities between a proton and the universe beyond our own galaxies, anticipated the concept of the Mandelbrot set.

The close tolerances and unrelenting constructional discipline demanded by a steel structure represent as much of a departure for Eames, who had hitherto used brick, as the concrete houses in Los Angeles were for Frank Lloyd Wright, who had previously built in wood and stone. They show a similar response to the elemental characteristics of the region by both architects, and an increasing tendency by Eames to impose additional restraints on himself. As Ralph Caplan has said in his essay 'Making Connections': 'one reason [why] Eames is so extremely sensitive to design restraints may be that

30

29

31

32

29 The plywood and steel spiral stair utilizes the same construction techniques found in the Eameses' furniture designs.
30 Minimal corner detailing allows the perception of continuous space, which characterizes the experience of the house from the interior, to be retained.
31 The kitchen, in the living segment of the house.
32 A sitting alcove, between the kitchen and the living area, was often also used for dining.

33

34

35

33 The studio, which began as a functioning work space, soon proved to be too small to contain the Eameses' widespread interests.

34 The Herman Miller Furniture showroom, designed at the same time as the Eames House, is one of Eames' largest commerical projects for an influential client.

35 The Revell Toy House designed for the Herman Miller Furniture Company to assist clients in space planning is a sophisticated toy, for adults.

36 Upper level rooms align with the ledge of the embankment into which the Eames House is carved.

37 In spite of the relatively modest size of many of the rooms in the house, the lightness of the steel frame, and minimal enclosure, prevent them from seeming claustrophobic.

38 Charles and Ray in the living space with some of the objects they collected, which personalize each room, in the foreground.

36

37

38

he has had so few conventional restraints imposed upon him'.[25] Because he and Ray were fortunate enough, through their talent, to be able to select the clients that they wanted to work with and the projects they were interested in being involved in, Caplan argues, Eames became his own most severe critic, and imposed a high level of discipline on himself. He quotes Eames as having said that 'if you are going to design for yourself, then you have to make sure you design deeply for yourself, because otherwise you are just designing for your eccentricities, and that's where you're different'.[26] Caplan concludes his views on the value of such selective abilities in Eames' work by saying that 'the rules of the game, in making a poem or a film or a way of life, do not require docile submission to restraints, only respect for them. Much of the tension in Eames' work comes from trying to push a material or an idea or a budget as far as it will go'.[27]

The Eames lounge chair, as a further example of such discipline, seems perfectly congruent with the Palisades house, in spite of the addition of luxurious leather, duck-down-filled cushions. An early, well-used specimen, which is still in the living room, and is purported to have been Charles' favourite chair, seems to fit in perfectly, because it is the result of the same structural logic as the house itself; an equally valid combination of the personal and the universal. It is this quality that Reyner Banham was referring to in

his own analysis of why the house had such an impact on architects in Europe when it appeared, particularly on those who were just beginning to formulate a new, mechanistic variant of Modernism, and how it revivified the movement, because it showed that the industrial ideal could have a human face.

The ability to establish this precarious balance of an architecture that answers to general principles, and yet accepts individual expression, evident in such diverse instances as the theme pavilions in Joseph Paxton's Crystal Palace and the Four Seasons Restaurant by Philip Johnson, where the status of the power brokers with assigned tables and private phones is enhanced rather than diminished or threatened by their surroundings, is a fragile thing, and, after Case Study #8 was completed, Charles Eames was never able to achieve it again. A furniture showroom for Herman Miller, which was designed at the same time as the Eameses' own house, and based on an almost identical module (but with a square rather than rectangular plan), has movable panels running in only one direction, making it a more active interpretation of the stationary walls of the house, which present an intentional rather than naturally changing display. While two walls of the orthogonal plan are steel and glass, the opposite two are brick, a vestigial reminder of Charles' earlier material preference, making the showroom appear to be a transitional work.

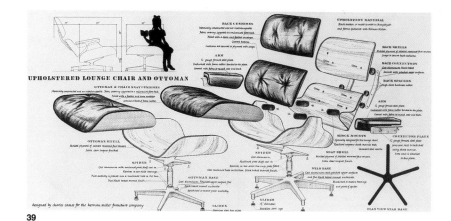

39

40

41

39 'The Eames Chair', Charles' most popular furniture design and his own personal favourite.
40 Graphics are rare in the house, and when used are given prominent positions.
41 Gauzy curtains allow more control of sunlight into the living area.

42

45

42 Eames' lounge chair,
seen here in the Eameses'
living room, has become a
contemporary classic of
modern design.
43 The Billy Wilder house.
44 The Kwikset house,
while never built, represents
an important conceptual
step for Charles Eames,
towards the high-tech ideal
of universal space.
45 The Entenza House,
adjacent to the Eames
House, has a totally
different profile from its
more visible neighbour.

43

44

Case Study House #9, which was also designed by Eames and Saarinen, for John Entenza, followed the Herman Miller project, but bears no resemblance to the crisp minimalism of its numerical predecessor or to the furniture showroom, which is its kinetic, commercial equivalent. While its structure is based on a similar network of 4in steel H-columns and 12in deep open web bar joists, the only structural members that are exposed are four of the 12 supporting steel columns, with birch strip ceiling and walls covering the rest.[28] The marked difference between the Eames and Entenza houses is the architects' effort to deliberately showcase the permutations allowed by the same industrial materials.

In the two years immediately following the completion of Case Study Houses #8 and #9, and the Herman Miller showroom, Charles and Ray Eames were involved in two other architectural projects, involving houses for Hollywood director Billy Wilder, as well as a prototype for the Kwikset Lock Company of Anaheim, California, but neither were realized. At 4,600 square feet, the Wilder residence was far more grandiose than his own, but Eames proposed a similar, minimalistic approach to the director, also based on the H-column and bar joist structure. The Kwikset House, on the other hand, was a departure from this system, since the roof of the single building, which was meant to continue the idea of developing an inexpensive prefabricated residence that could be rapidly assembled from readily available parts, was made up of curved plywood roof sections, supported by laminated plywood beams and a modular metal frame. Room divisions inside the open, hanger-like space were provided by 8ft high storage units, with placement decided by each owner, and services were grouped along the exterior walls from which the plywood roof sprang. In spite of the fact that it fulfilled all contract requirements, a change in company ownership forced cancellation of the Kwikset project.[29] As a result of these disappointments, as well as his general disillusionment with what he called the 'frustrating business' of architecture, late in 1951 Eames decided to concentrate exclusively on furniture design, as well as on exhibitions and films, making Case Study #8 the most important tectonic achievement of his career.

The significance of the Eames House

In retrospect, the loss of the Kwikset commission was critical for Eames, not only because it broke the momentum of construction that had begun in 1949, eventually leading to a decision to abandon architecture altogether, but also because it blocked the growth of a theoretical idea begun in Pacific Palisades. The direction of this process, which may now be recognized as leading to the realization of a high-tech model, suggests that Case Study #8 be placed at the beginning, rather than the end of the

46

47

46 The steel projection of the Entenza House acts as a shading device for a large window.
47 The roof itself, with the glass wall recessed behind it, acts as an integrated device for reducing glare on the elevation of the Entenza House that faces the sea.
48 An early photograph from the Entenza House looking towards the Eames House, shows the visual relationship between them and the need for the eucalyptus screen planted by the Eameses for privacy.

curve, in the compressed period of ideological evolution that the architect experienced between the announcement of the 'Bridge House' in the January 1945 issue of *Arts & Architecture* and the cancellation of the Wilder project in 1951. Its position near the start of that six-year cycle makes the Eames House the exception that proves the rules toward which its designer was gravitating and also helps to explain its unprecedented influence.

In both form and concept, the Kwikset House, with its single span made possible by the soft technology of laminated beams and plywood roofs, anticipates later and larger examples in the same genre, which also rely on a central, unobstructed space and grouping of services at the perimeter, but in more aggressive materials. Beyond its most obvious statement, as an attempt to expand on the idea of total prefabrication, off-the-shelf cost reductions and a surrogate for solid wood that Eames seemed to feel comfortable with because of his familiarity with it, the Kwikset prototype shows a growing commitment to the high-tech myth of unobstructed flexibility, which has now resulted in, for example, the spectacular structural pyrotechnics of the Hongkong & Shanghai Bank by Foster, the Pompidou Centre by Piano and Rogers, and the Lloyd's Building by Rogers.

The Eames House, by contrast, is relatively compartmentalized and, with its service and utility cores placed inwards towards the central court in both its living and studio segments, it inverts the configuration of the Herman Miller showroom and Kwikset House. In its close relationship to its site, the house also contradicts the high-tech tendency to reject context as the obvious corollary to concentration on one grand interior span. The Eames House is literally and figuratively wedded to the land, and fully responsive to its variations, rather than remaining aloof from them, as the preliminary 'Bridge House' would have. The decision to swing the free-standing bridge around in a 90° arc, from an elevated position above the meadow to the retaining wall at its edge, was ostensibly motivated by a wish not to seem derivative; and yet the conceptual shift is so significant that this alone does not satisfactorily answer the question of intent. The Mies drawing Eames had seen at MoMA is a quick, freehand sketch, and while it is virtually identical to Contini's original *parti*, the likelihood of basing such a major change on this small sketch alone, especially after the steel had already been ordered, seems improbable. For all of his admiration for Buckminster Fuller and Jean Prouvé, in 1948 Eames was not yet ready to implement fully high modern principles, and a quasi-conventional *Raumplan* is the result. Like Loos, who sought to retain the best of the past, while also making use of the latest technological advances, Eames seems to have been initially reluctant to abandon the seductive prerogatives of 'design'.

49

49, 50 Entenza House, the living room area with its freestanding fireplace as its focal point, and a bedroom alcove beyond.
51, 52 Entenza House, bathroom and kitchen.

50

51

52

53 Using a similar strategy to that employed at the Entenza House, the Eameses recessed the glass facing the sea beneath an overhanging roof.
54 Working drawings of the Eames House show the steel framing plan supplied by the engineer Contini.

53

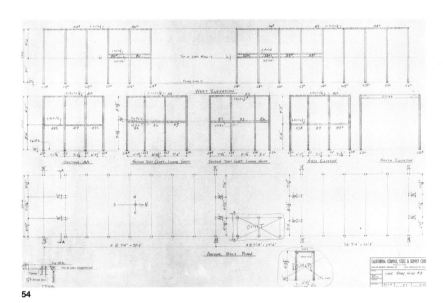

54

In an article for the July 1944 issue of *Arts & Architecture* written jointly by Charles Eames and John Entenza, which preceded the Bridge House by one year, the authors argue that any architect who wants to design a truly successful prefabricated house must first become a student of human behaviour, as well as science, economics and industrial engineering. 'The value of the house that results from such a combination,' they say, 'will be measured by the degree to which it serves for the amount of energy it costs. The relation of service to price is so important that nothing can justifiably be added to the house that does not increase its value in service'.[30] Directly addressing the question of what service is, they continue by saying that 'the degrees of service are real and can be measured; they are not dependent on taste. If this is true this is a house which will not alter itself by architectural design'.[31] 'Service', by this definition, contradicts the distinction first popularized by Louis Kahn, and eloquently implemented by James Stirling, between 'served' and 'servant' spaces, standing instead as a synonym for the activities of daily life rather than the support systems that facilitate them.

The basic paradox of the Eames House, as it was finally realized, revolved around this confusion in terms, and makes its enthusiastic international reception by ultra-modernists even more ironic. It is hard to imagine the production of 'thousands' of this

same design, as Eames and Entenza advocated in their article on the ideal prefabricated house, because it 'served' its owners' special interests as well, and it is this particularly, in the guise of a prefabricated ideal, that is the basis of its popular appeal. The high-tech fantasy of off-the-shelf parts which Eames sought to perpetuate by proclaiming costs that were ten times less than those for conventional, balloon-frame construction, is just as much an exercise in self-deception as it has proven to be in other, equally iconographic attempts at standardization, where customized adaptations were finally found to be necessary. Published costs of $1.00 per square foot, in comparison to $11.50 for wood framing at that time, conveniently overlook the additional hours spent in furnishing and fit-out by members of the Eames office staff, which were not added into the cost.[32] The much-vaunted construction time of one-and-a-half days, which is certainly remarkable, and did translate directly into a valuable cost-benefit, should be re-evaluated against this additional labour, as well as Eames' own criterion that the value of the house should be measured by 'the energy it costs'. In the wider view of architects pursuing sustainable values today, who believe that the amount of energy used to produce or manufacture a material must also be considered as a factor in its selection, his statement now seems prescient, but his choice of steel does not.

The Japanese influence

In a final non-parallel with high-tech dogma, there are historical references in the house, albeit abstracted, that tie to a succession of a well-established precedents in foreshortened, Los Angeles time, which are all related to the Japanese attitude toward interior and exterior space. The influence of the Japanese exhibition and the Ho-o-den Temple at the Columbian Exposition in Chicago in 1893 has been well documented, and the Gamble House in Pasadena by Charles and Henry Greene is the first and most complete synthesis of its transfer to southern California. With its wide, overhanging hipped roofs, loving respect for material and detail, uncluttered interiors and sensitive interrelationship with its natural surroundings, the Gamble House may be seen to have irrefutable roots across the Pacific, as does the Bay tradition, which is a parallel, further north.

As unlikely as any ideological similarities with Frank Lloyd Wright may initially seem, he also used the Ho-o-den Temple as a model for his Prairie houses, in similar ways, before carrying the same ideas over into the Barnsdall House, in Los Angeles, in a new medium and context. The stucco-covered wooden frame of this house, which was detailed to simulate concrete, may hardly be described as an essay in truth to materials, due to Wright's determined attempt to break visually and emotionally with his Oak Park past. But he is now recognized as having been one of the most knowledgeable connoisseurs of Japanese art and architecture in the United States at the time Barnsdall House was built, with an extensive personal collection that he made available to clients, for sale. His use of the ritual tokonoma and its appropriate statue, which Aline Barnsdall bought from him to place at the entrance to Barnsdall House, as well as his customarily adroit handling of the processional sequence that it initiates, are evident enough, but only minor connections to Eastern tradition compared to the subtle alignment with physical elements that slowly becomes evident when moving through the house. His reading of them makes his work on Olive Hill an anagram for the climatic extremes that are singular to this region. Wright's subsequent commission for the Imperial Hotel in Tokyo, as well as for several private residences around the city, echo both the configuration and style of Barnsdall House, and confirm his intentions there. The use of a central court, in particular, which was evidently included at Aline Barnsdall's insistence, and then appropriated by Wright as his own, extends the exterior connections that were so carefully orchestrated by Greene and Greene into another dimension, with parallels in classic Japanese examples, such as the Katsura Palace, where inside and outside blend into one. A similar kind of spatial inversion operates throughout

55

56

55 The Gamble House (1907–8) by Greene and Greene, while seemingly quite different in style from the Eames House, reflects a similar attitude towards the relationship between interior and exterior space.
56 The Barnsdall House (1921) by Frank Lloyd Wright, is organized around a central court, as are the living and working areas of the Eames House.
57 Cross bracing provides structural stability for an exceptionally thin steel frame, as well as an effective visual foil to the orthogonal grid of the main elevation.

Barnsdall House, in spite of the difference in the thickness of its walls, but is most successful in the central atrium overlooking the court, where Wright used glass. Rudolph Schindler, who arrived in America from Austria just prior to the First World War (and before Richard Neutra who emigrated a few years later in 1923), became project manager at Olive Hill while Wright was in Tokyo. The deep impression that Wright's extensive collection of artefacts had on Schindler while he had served as an apprentice at Taliesin in Wisconsin, was nurtured during his time at Barnsdall House, where he was exposed to the essential relationships behind the building's controversial forms.

When the time came for him to build his own house on Kings Road, Los Angeles in 1922, using prefabricated concrete tilt-slab construction, Schindler attempted a similar kind of spatial penetration, adding a second court for another family that was to share the house with him and his wife. While the tilt-up slabs with gaps between them to let in light, form a hard, outer perimeter, the inner skin of the walls facing the courts are made up of sliding white canvas panels in a wooden frame, reminiscent of the shoji screens of Japanese houses. Richard Neutra's Case Study efforts with which Eames was certainly familiar, were themselves patterned on the ingenious, protective spiral of the Kings Road plan, which provided optimum exposure to the gardens, trees and lawn.

The stripped down, minimalist interiors of the Case Study series, put forward as a modern alternative to the cluttered and compartmentalized pre-Second World War American house, were meant to allow returning veterans and their families a more casual lifestyle, in a climate that is most conducive to it. This idea, however, was not new, since, even before the end of the 19th century, the Japanese attitude to decoration was seen as valuing restraint as opposed to the ostentation of late-Victorian and Edwardian taste in the west, using natural materials, simple forms, and playing with light and shadow rather than pattern and ornament, inducing calm and contemplation.

While the Japanese equation is still an important aspect of many of the most well-known architects practising in Los Angeles today, such as Frank Gehry, Thom Mayne of Morphosis, Eric Owen Moss and Frank Israel, it is significant that the transfer has changed around completely to an emphasis on artificial rather than natural similarities. Paradoxically, these architects, who are considered to be trend-setters elsewhere, now regard Japan as the origin of innovation, the place to watch for new ideas, an urban soul mate beleaguered by similar problems, and subjected to comparable growing pains, which forces it to be equally creative in attempting to find solutions.

58

59

60

58 The Japanese inspiration for the house carried over into the Eameses' social life, as shown in this photograph of a dinner party in honour of Charlie Chaplin, who can be seen here in the centre of the front row.

59, 60 The composition of glass panes and solid wall panels was devised to create interesting patterns of light in the interior.

61 Case Study House #16, Bel Air, 1953 by Craig Ellwood.

62 Case Study House #21, Laurel Canyon, 1958 by Pierre Koenig.

63 Raphael Soriano, seen here on site at his Case Study House (unnumbered), 1950.

61

62

63

The Edo ideals of purity, humility and oneness with nature that captivated the Greene brothers and Frank Lloyd Wright are distilled in the Eames House for the last time making it a bench-mark of that tradition in the city. From that point forward, it is the mastery of technology alone, rather than mystical notions about submission to natural laws that has been the envy of Los Angeles architects; and yet it has continued to captivate successive generations there, not because it is a modular re-interpretation of the Tatami generated palaces of Japan's classic period, but because it is built in steel, and improbably and almost magically balances strength with lightness. Following the Eames House, there was a dramatic shift in the character of the Case Study houses, which had predominantly been built in wood before it appeared. Raphael Soriano, for example, designed a residence that was built one mile north of Case Study houses #8 and #9, and opened to the public as part of Entenza's programme in 1950. As described by Ray Eames, with John and Marilyn Neuhart, the house was an important step for Soriano, who 'had become interested in steel when he worked in the early 1930s in Neutra's office; although Neutra used it rarely after his 1929 Lovell House use, Soriano took it up from there and made it a life pursuit'.[33]

He was soon joined by other Case Study architects such as Craig Ellwood and Pierre Koenig, who continued to refine the concept of the steel house still further, until it became evident that American construction methods were too deeply ingrained to adapt to such a radical change, and trade unions were reluctant to endorse prefabricated housing because they felt it might threaten jobs. The revolution in domestic architecture which Charles and Ray Eames envisaged never came about because industry was not ready to accept such an idea, and the public was put off by the thought of living in sterile, steel and glass pavilions. For all the democratic pronouncements made in *Arts & Architecture*, the Case Study projects, and the Eames House in particular, were intended for a select few. 'The Style that Nearly Was', as Reyner Banham has called it, was ahead of its time, and aimed at the wrong market.[34] The renewed interest in steel as a building material, paralleling the obsession with fitness and self-defence that is now endemic in Los Angeles, is symptomatic of a response to life in a city that now seems to be growing with no direction, out of control. The 'Blade Runner scenario', as it is so often called, after Ridley Scott's classic movie of the same name, depicts the future city as a violent, chaotic urban jungle, and is considered by many sociologists to have already come about. The recent popularity of heavy metal among many architects there shows that Eames was prophetic in his choice of materials. Wright, who was more sensitive than most to natural prerequisites, reached instinctively to the climatic extremes of southern California, where everything happens in excess. Rain, when it intermittently interrupts the almost constant sunshine, tends to be torrential, and earthquakes occur with disturbing frequency. Snow-capped mountains form an almost unbroken backdrop to the wide expanse of ocean, the blue line of America's furthest westward expansion, before Hawaii was made a state. Wright's response to this was mass alone, followed by concrete, and recourse to what he simply called 'the machine'. In Pacific Palisades, where such extremes are even more violent, Eames also chose a durable material, tempered with elegance.

Following his failure to complete the Billy Wilder and Kwikset houses, which would have allowed him to expand the idiom first put forward in Case Study #8, Charles Eames turned to the production of complex exhibitions, in addition to furniture design and film work. From the time of his initial efforts with Eero Saarinen, in their joint production of an exhibition of faculty work at Cranbrook, Eames had a growing interest in such design, and they became increasingly more involved over time. One of the most spectacular of these was 'The World of Franklin and Jefferson', which his office produced for the American Revolution Bicentennial Administration. It was a travelling exhibition that opened at the Metropolitan Museum of Art in March 1976, on a theme with which Eames was already quite familiar, having been commissioned by the United States Information Agency to prepare a presentation on Thomas Jefferson in 1973, when he put forward the idea of comparing the former president to statesman and inventor Benjamin Franklin.[35] The first three segments of the four-part show were respectively titled 'Friends and Acquaintances', 'Contrast and Continuity', and 'Three Documents'; the fourth, called 'Jefferson and the West', focused mainly on the executive involvement in the Louisiana Purchase. One of Eames' personal commandments, repeated in the fifth lecture of the Norton series, delivered in 1971, was not to take any job 'with whose objectives you do not agree'.[36] The Franklin and Jefferson exhibition, which took place only two years before his death in August 1978, at the age of 71, had objectives which most certainly must have been in concert with a man whose self-image was that of a Yankee inventor in the best tradition of these two prestigious predecessors. The innovation apparent in the Eames House can be traced, in a straight line, back to the empirical adaptations made on American clipper ships, to increase their speed, in order to survive in a competitive market. While the motives behind Case Study #8 were not entirely commercial, it is undoubtedly a part of this legacy, and along with the Franklin and Jefferson exhibition, it remains the most accurate record of the values and talent of a complex man.

64 The Eames House represents a close collaboration between Charles and Ray, reflecting their individual personalities and interests. They cooperated throughout their life together on everything the Eames Office produced – the Eames House is the culmination of that partnership.

64

Photographs

Previous page and left
The eucalyptus trees,
originally planted as a screen
to provide privacy between
the Eames and Entenza
houses, have now grown to
such an extent that they
almost completely obscure
the Eames House.

Left and centre The corrugated metal decking, generally considered to be a cheap commercial material, forms an exposed soffit on the west elevation of the house, conveying a sense of elegance.
Right A thin section bar joist, supporting the projection over the western facade, accentuates the repetitive ribbing of the soffit.

Left Corner detailing in such a minimalist assembly takes on exaggerated importance. Eames, like Mies van der Rohe, understood the importance of restraint and scale in subtle detailing.
Right Syncopated graduation of panel sizes accentuate the vertical expression of the facade.

In stark contrast to the restrictive industrial tolerances of steel construction, the gnarled tree trunks outside are a reminder of the organic randomness of nature.

Charles and Ray Eames
took constant pleasure in
the smallest details of
nature surrounding the
house, and captured many
of them, such as the
shimmering reflection of the
leaves in the glass panes,
on film.

Left and centre In a similar device to that used by Frank Lloyd Wright, constricted entrances lead to lofty open areas with generous exterior views. **Right** When the Eames House was first published its impact was considerable, as it showed that Modernism, which had reached its zenith, could, after all, be personalized.

The collections of the Eameses included a diverse library of objects brought back from their extensive travels. This eclectic assemblage reduces the pronounced scale of the living and working spaces to human proportions.

The bedroom (above) and
bedroom hallway (left).
Private spaces, such as
these, on the first floor,
achieve privacy by partition
walls that are similar in
character to the shoji
screens in traditional
Japanese houses.

The kitchen contains furniture designed by the Eameses, providing an example of the modern ideal of integrated disciplines. Even the kitchen cabinet surfaces are personalized by Ray's collection of objects.

The courtyard between the
living and working spaces
was originally intended to
have a screen wall,
simulating an arcade
connecting each area. This
was quickly eliminated to
beneficial effect.

The studio or working space is more utilitarian in character than the living space, with a steel ladder stairway leading up to the mezzanine level. A sliding glass door leads directly to the driveway.

On approaching the house, the studio elevation (far right) appears to be more unified and substantial than the other elevations, with mullion configurations (above) reminiscent of Schindler's Kings Road House, continuing this impression of closure. Suspended shelving (right) provides additional display space for the models used in the Eameses' films which were produced in the studio.

A limited palette of
materials, including steel
and glass, show the
effectiveness of a restrained
approach to detailing.

Location map
1 Eames House
2 drive
3 flood control channel
4 Entenza House

Drawings

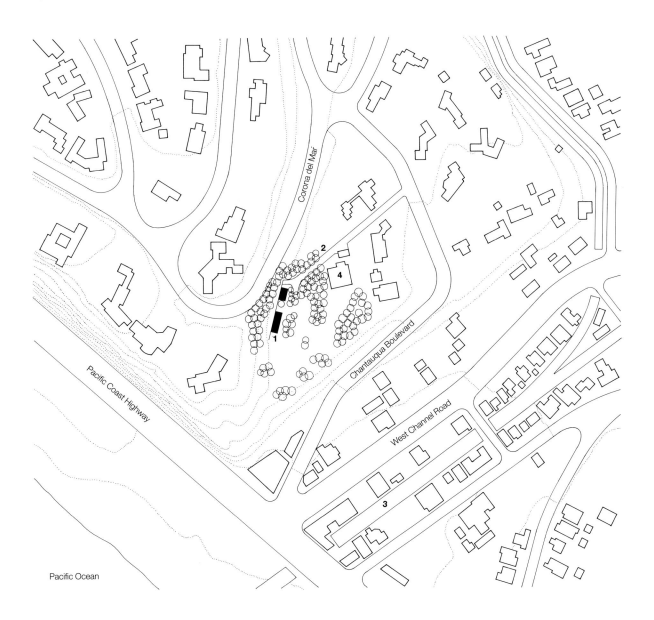

Corona del Mar

Chantauqua Boulevard

Pacific Coast Highway

West Channel Road

Pacific Ocean

0   50m

0   150ft

Floor plans

1 living room
2 dining room
3 kitchen
4 utility room
5 upper part of living
  room
6 bedroom
7 dressing alcove/room
8 hall
9 bathroom
10 courtyard
11 studio
12 dark room
13 upper part of studio
14 storage deck

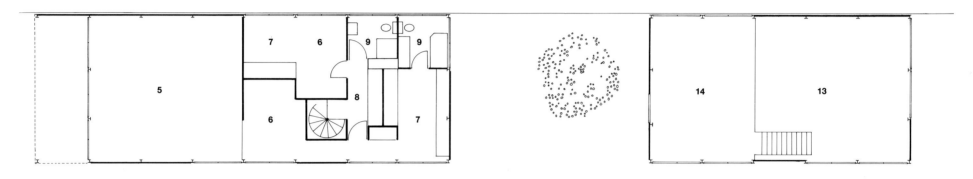

First floor

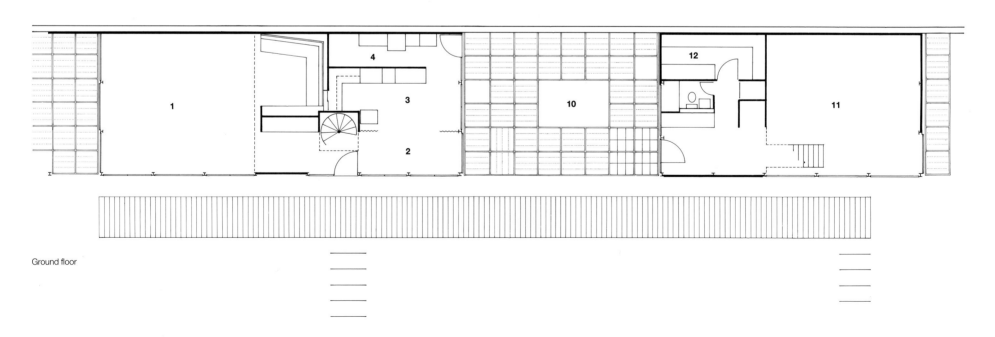

Ground floor

0   3m

0   10ft

Cross section

0   500mm

0   18in

House: north elevation

House: south elevation

Elevations

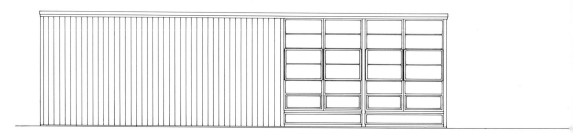

West elevation

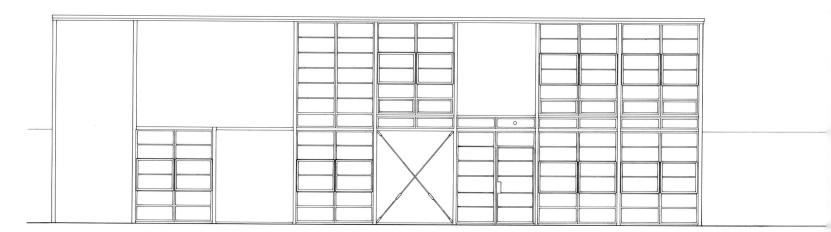

East elevation

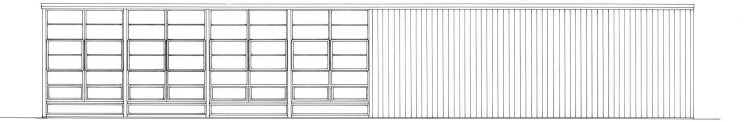
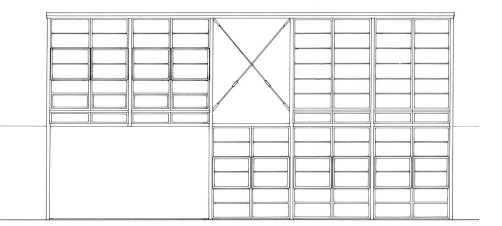

Studio: north elevation

0   500mm

0   18in

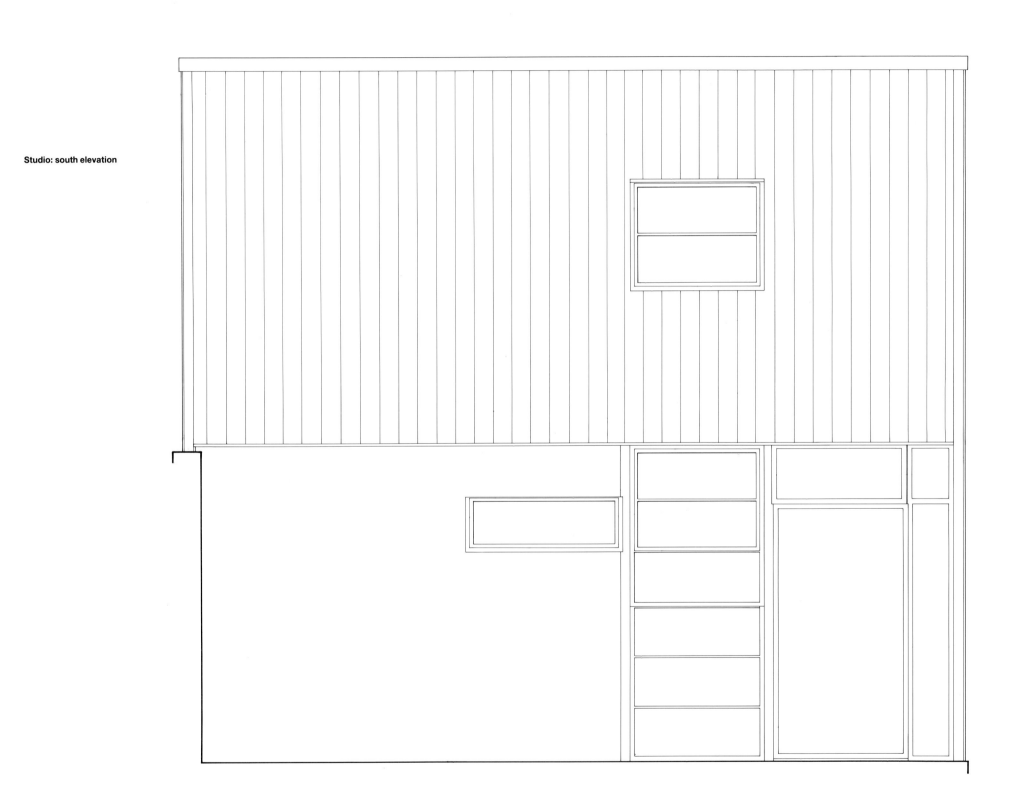

Studio: south elevation

Detailed wall
section/plan

1   gravel surface on built-up roof
2   metal gravel stop and fascia flashing
3   0.43in (12.5mm) insulation board
4   1.75in (44.45 mm) FER-ROBOARD steel decking
5   3x3x0.17in (76.2x76.2x4.2mm) continuous steel angle
6   12in (304.8mm) fabricated steel joist
7   0.38in (9.5mm) steel plate joist connection bolted to columns using 0.5in (12.7mm) diameter bolts
8   4x4in (101.6x101.6mm) steel column
9   steel window frame welded to structure and glazed with: double strength glass; polished wired glass; polished plate glass; obscured glass; or opaque panel, depending on location
10 finished first floor level
11 4x3x0.19in (101.6x76.2x4.8mm) continuous steel angle
12 14in (355.6mm) fabricated steel joist
13 finished ceiling line
14 flashing
15 12in (304.8mm) steel channel
16 10.5x4.5x0.25in (266.7x114.3x6.35mm) steel plate connection bolted to column
17 lath and plaster on 0.75in (19mm) timber stripping
18 finished ground floor level
19 3.5in (88.9mm) concrete slab
20 waterproof membrane
21 5x5x5in (127x127x12.7mm) steel base plate bolted to concrete foundation using 0.626in (15.9mm) diameter x 10in (254mm) bolts

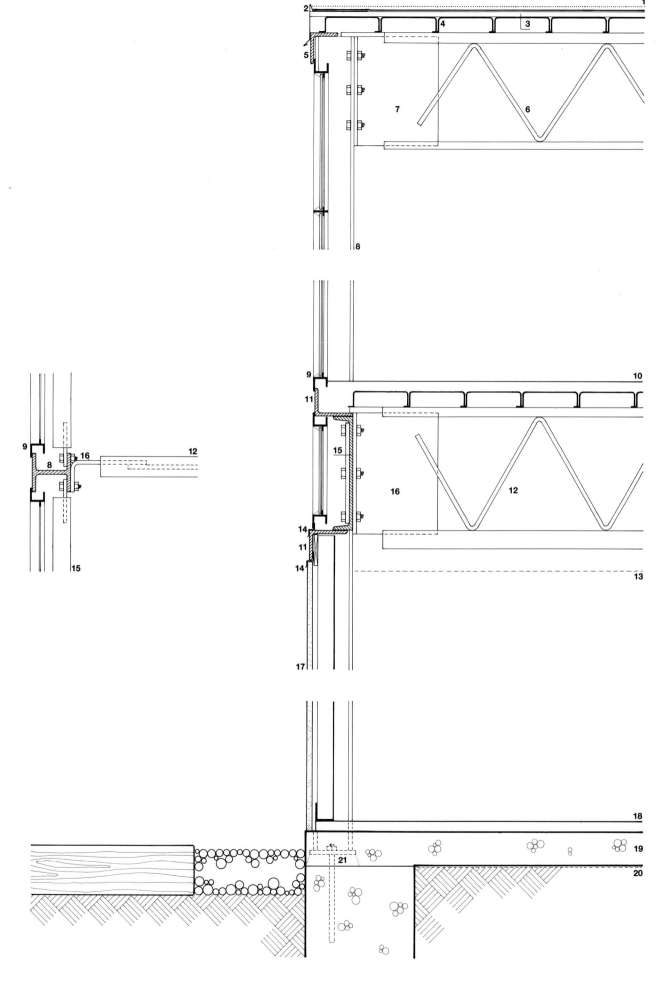

0   200mm

0   8in

Stair

1 3.5in (88.9mm) diameter steel tube with open end

2 fabricated steel bracket

3 finished tread line (1.13in (28.6mm) plywood treads not shown)

4 1.38in (35mm) steel base plate bolted to concrete slab

5 3in (76.2mm) diameter x 120in (3048mm) tube welded to base plate

6 step no 5

7 step no 14

8 0.5in (12.2mm) bolt hole

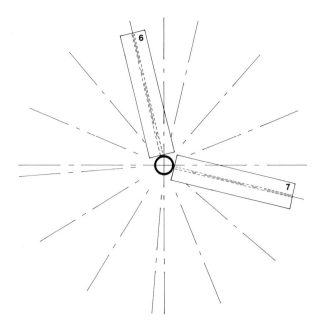

Plan

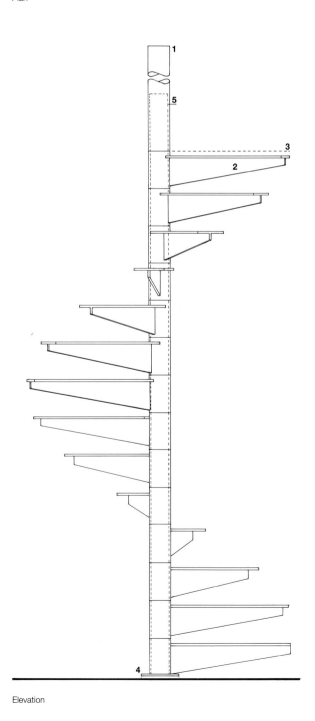

Elevation

Plan and elevation of step

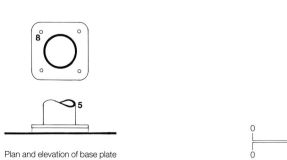

Plan and elevation of base plate

0   300mm

0   12in

0   150mm

0   6in

Acknowledgements

The author wishes to thank Aristos Demetrios, Lucia Eames Demetrios, Eames Demetrios, Shelley Mills and Jo Newson for their help towards the completion of this book.

Illustrations were provided with the kind permission of the following: Eames Office, figs 1–3, 5–7, 9, 11–24, 33–35, 39, 42–44, 54, 57, 58, 64; Julius Shulman, figs 4–8, 25–32, 36–38, 40, 41, 45–53, 59, 60, 62–64; Peter Aprahamian, fig 61; Tim Street-Porter, figs 55, 56.

Notes

1 John Neuhart, Marilyn Neuhart and Ray Eames, *Eames Design: The Work of the Office of Charles and Ray Eames* (London: Thames and Hudson, 1989), p 17.
2 ibid, p 19.
3 ibid, p 22.
4 Knights of Columbus, Helena Council #1770, *The Art and Architecture of St Mary's Catholic Church* (church pamphlet), Helena, Arkansas, 1986, p 2.
5 *Eames Design*, p 22.
6 ibid, p 25.
7 ibid, p 49.
8 ibid, p 26.
9 ibid, p 26.
10 ibid, p 26.
11 ibid, p 47.
12 ibid, p 49.
13 ibid, p 107.
14 ibid, p 49.
15 ibid, p 49.
16 ibid, p 107.
17 ibid, p 107.
18 ibid, p 137.
19 ibid, p 110.
20 ibid, p 199.
21 ibid, p 110.
22 ibid, p 199.
23 ibid, p 199.
24 ibid, p 235.
25 Ralph Caplan, John Neuhart and Marilyn Neuhart, *Connections: The Work of Charles and Ray Eames* (exhibition catalogue), Los Angeles: UCLA, Los Angeles Art Center, 1976, p 29.
26 ibid, p 30.
27 ibid, p 32.
28 *Eames Design*, p 123.
29 ibid, p 155.
30 ibid, p 47.
31 ibid, p 47.
32 ibid, p 109.
33 ibid, p 109.
34 Esther McCoy et al, *Blueprints for Modern Living: History and Legacy of the Case Study Houses*, Los Angeles: Museum of Contemporary Art, 1990, p 183.
35 *Eames Design*, p 391.
36 ibid, p 360.

Bibliography

'Abitazione Studio, Santa Monica, CA', *L'Architecture d'Aujourd'hui*, vol 24, nos 50–1, December 1953, pp 114–5.

Architectural Design (issue on Charles and Ray Eames), vol 36, no 9, September 1966, pp 458–70.

Architectural Review, vol 110, no 658, October 1951, pp 230–31.

Architectural Review, vol 189, no 1129, March 1991, pp 27–78 (special issue, 'Working Places: Problems and Opportunities').

Baroni, Daniele, 'Charles Eames and the Methodology of Design', *Ottagono*, vol 16, no 61, June 1981, pp 18–85 (text in Italian, with an English summary).

Best, Alastair, 'Charles Eames', *Architects' Journal*, vol 168, no 41, 11 October 1978, pp 669–71.

Carolin, Peter, 'Domestic High-tech', *Bauwelt*, vol 78, no 20, 1987, pp 714–17 (text in German).

Carpenter, Edward, *Industrial Design: 25th Annual Design in Review* (New York: Whitney Library of Design, 1979) (Introduction: A Tribute to Charles Eames).

'Casa Estudio en California 38', *Arquitectura*, June 1952, pp 153–6.

'Case Study Houses 8 and 9 by Charles Eames and Eero Saarinen', *Arts & Architecture*, December 1945, pp 43–57.

'Case Study Houses 8 and 9', *Arts & Architecture*, vol 65, March 1948, pp 40–41.

'Case Study House Number 9 Under Construction', *Arts & Architecture*, vol 66, no 1, January 1949, pp 31–2.

'Case Study House for 1949', *Arts & Architecture*, vol 66, no 2, February 1949, p 37.

'Case Study House for 1949: The Steel Frame', *Arts & Architecture*, vol 66, no 3, March 1949, pp 30–1.

'Case Study House for 1949: The Plan', *Arts & Architecture*, vol 66, no 5, May 1949, pp 38–9.

'Case Study House for 1949: The Interiors', *Arts & Architecture*, vol 66, no 9, September 1949, p 33.

'Case Study House for 1949', *Arts & Architecture*, vol 66, no 12, December 1949, pp 26–39.

'Case Study House by Eames and Saarinen', *Arts & Architecture*, vol 67, no 7, July 1950, pp 26–39.

'Charles Eames, 1907–1978', *Bauen und Wohnen*, vol 33, no 12, 1978, pp 490–1 (text in English, French and German).

'Charles Eames: 1907–1978', *Interior Design*, vol 49, no 10, 1978, pp 234–5.

'Charles Eames' forward-looking furniture', *Magazine of Art*, vol 39, May 1946, pp 179–81.

'Charles Eames: habitation et atelier, Santa Monica, Cal.', *L'Architecture d'Aujourd'hui*, no 50, 1953.

Collins, Michael, *Towards Post-Modernism: Design since 1851* (London: British Museum Publications, 1987) (biographical section).

Dixon, John Morris et al, 'Interior design', *Progressive Architecture*, vol 71, no 9, September 1990, pp 95–136.

Diffrient, Niels, 'Good goods', *Progressive Architecture*, vol 71, no 9, September 1990, pp 142 and 190.

Domus, no 402, May 1963 (special issue on Eames).

Drexler, Arthur, *Charles Eames: Furniture from the Design Collection* (New York: The Museum of Modern Art, 1973).

Dunster, David (ed) *Key Buildings in the Twentieth Century, vol 2: Houses 1945–1989* (London: Butterworth, 1990).

'The Eames aesthetic', *Canadian Architect*, vol 18, no 6, June 1973, pp 56–9.

'An Eames celebration', *Architecture SA 11*, summer 1980, pp 33–7.

Eames, Charles, 'Organic Design', *Arts & Architecture*, December 1941.

Eames, Charles, 'A Prediction, Less Self-Expression for the Designer', *Print*, vol 14, no 1, January–February 1960, pp 77–9.

'Eames at Home', *Architectural Forum*, vol 138, no 3, April 1973, pp 71–2.

'Eames House' (AIA Award), *Progressive Architecture*, vol 59, no 4, 1978, pp 33 and 36.

Emery, Marc, *Furniture by Architects: 500 International Masterpieces of Twentieth-Century Design and Where to Buy Them* (New York: Abrams, 1983, expanded edition 1988).

Fehrman, Cherie and Fehrman, Kenneth, *Post-War Interior Design 1945–1960* (New York: Van Nostrand Reinhold, 1987).

Gill, Brendan, *The Dream Come True: Great Houses of Los Angeles* (New York: Lippincott and Crowell, 1980).

Goldstein, Barbara, Lee, Charles and Polyzoides, Stefanos, 'The Eames House', *Arts & Architecture*, vol 2, no 2, February 1983, pp 20–5.

Graf, Douglas, 'Strange siblings – being and nothingness: an inadvertent homage to Ray and Charles Eames', *Datutop*, no 14, 1991, pp 1–71.

Harris, Frank and Bonenberger, Weston (eds), *A Guide to Contemporary Architecture in Southern California* (Los Angeles: Watling and Co, 1951).

McCoy, Esther, 'Arts & Architecture Case Study Houses', *Perspecta*, no 15, 1975, pp 54–73.

McCoy, Esther et al, *Blueprints for Modern Living: History and Legacy of the Case Study Houses*, Los Angeles: Museum of Contemporary Art, 1990 (published on the occasion of an exhibition held at the Museum of Contemporary Art, 17 October 1988–18 February 1990).

McCoy, Esther, *Case Study Houses 1945–1962* (Los Angeles: Hennessey and Ingalls Inc, 1977).

McCoy, Esther, 'Charles and Ray Eames', *Design Quarterly*, nos 98–9, 1975, pp 20–9 and 58–9.

McCoy, Esther, *Modern California Houses: Case Study Houses 1945–1962* (New York: Reinhold Publishing Corporation, 1962).

McKean, John Maule, 'The Two Great Heroes: an Interview with Charles and Ray Eames', *Building Design*, no 267, 26 September 1975, pp 12–13.

Morrison, Philip and Phylis, and the Office of Charles and Ray Eames, *Powers of Ten: About the Relative Size of Things in the Universe* (San Francisco: Scientific American Library vol 1, W H Freeman and Co, 1982).

Mulard, Claudine, 'Studios Bright', *Architecture Intérieure Crée*, no 241, February/March 1991, pp 108–13 (text in French, summaries in English).

Naylor, Colin (ed), *Contemporary Masterworks* (Chicago and London: St James Press, 1991).

Neuhart, John and Neuhart, Marilyn, *Connections: The Work of Charles and Ray Eames* (exhibition catalogue), Los Angeles: UCLA/Los Angeles Art Council, 1976.

Neuhart, John, Neuhart, Marilyn and Eames, Ray, *Eames Design: The Work of the Office of Charles and Ray Eames* (London: Thames and Hudson, 1989).

Page, Marian, *Furniture Designed by Architects*. (New York: Whitney Library of Design, 1980).

Ponti, Lisa Licitra, 'Charles Eames: More than a Designer, 1907–1978', *Domus*, no 587, October 1978.

'Prologue', *Progressive Architecture*, vol 52, no 7, July 1971, pp 56–9.

Rubino, Luciano, 'Il Rifugio della Natura: Uno prototipo: La Casa-Studio di Ray e Charles Eames', *Ville e Giardini*, no 147, July/August 1980.

Rubino, Luciano, *Ray e Charles Eames: Il Collettivo Della Fantasia* (Rome: Edizioni Kappa, 1981).

Saatchi, Doris, 'All about Eames', *House and Garden*, vol 156, February 1984, pp 122–31.

Silvy, Maurice, 'La Maison de Charles et Ray Eames à Los Angeles', *L'Architecture d'Aujourd'hui*, vol 33, no 103, September 1962, pp 31–2.

Smithson, Alison and Peter (eds), 'Eames Celebration', *Architectural Design*, vol 36, no 9 (special issue on Charles and Ray Eames), pp 432–42.

Smithson, Peter, 'Charles Eames: 1907–1978', *RIBA Journal*, vol 85, no 10, October 1978.

Steinmann, Martin et al, 'Interior design', *Archithese*, vol 13, no 1, January 1983, pp 3–36 (text in German, English summary).

Sudjic, Deyan, 'One man and his Museum', *Blueprint*, no 62, November 1989, pp 38–52.

Visconti, Marco, 'Quattro Case Sperimentali', *Domus*, no 711, December 1989, pp 72–84.

Wallace, Don, 'Design Laboratory for Industrial Innovation: Charles Eames', *Industrial Design*, vol 3, no 4, August 1956, pp 88–90.

'What is Design?', *Progressive Architecture*, vol 71, no 2, February 1990, p 122 (excerpts from a 1969 interview with Charles Eames).

Chronology

1945

Case Study House programme first announced in January, in the *Arts & Architecture* magazine; first design, 'Bridge House', published in December

1947

After a visit to exhibition of Mies van der Rohe's works at the Museum of Modern Art, New York, Charles Eames revises his plans

1949

Construction begins with excavations in January; second and final design published in the *Arts & Architecture* magazine in May. Frames of the house erected in one and a half days, or 90 man-hours. Charles and Ray Eames move in on Christmas Eve, 1949

3 ARCHITECTURE **s**

TWENTIETH-CENTURY HOUSES

Beth Dunlop is the former architecture critic of the *Miami Herald* and currently writes on architecture for a variety of publications.
Denis Hector is an associate professor at the University of Miami School of Architecture where he is also Director of graduate programmes.

Frank Lloyd Wright
Fallingwater

Robert McCarter is a practising architect and Professor and Chair of the Department of Architecture, University of Florida. He has written for numerous architectural publications and he was the founding editor of the journals *Abstract* and *Constructions*. His previous books include *Building: Machines* 1987, *Frank Lloyd Wright: A Primer on Architectural Principles* 1991 and *Frank Lloyd Wright* 1997, also published by Phaidon Press.

Alvar Aalto
Villa Mairea

Richard Weston is Head of the School of Architecture at Portsmouth Polytechnic. He is an authority on the architecture of Finland in general and the work of Alvar Aalto in particular. He is also a prize-winning writer – author of *Alvar Aalto* and *Säynätsalo Town Hall* in the Architecture in Detail series, both published by Phaidon – and a regular contributor to the *Architects' Journal* and the *Architectural Review*.

Acknowledgements The author and the publisher are grateful to Professor Juhani Pallasmaa and the Villa Mairea Foundation for their permission to use photographs of the Villa Mairea in this book.

The author and draughtsman, Darren Stewart Capel, wish to acknowledge the invaluable help and co-operation of Mrs Elissa Aalto, members of the Alvar Aalto and Company office, which she directs, and the Aalto Archive throughout the preparation of this study.

Charles and Ray Eames
Eames House

James Steele has taught and practiced architecture in Philadelphia and in Saudi Arabia. He has been guest lecturer at Texas Tech University, writes frequently for the *Architectural Review* and *Architectural Design* magazines, and is currently Visiting Professor at the University of Southern California in Los Angeles. He is an important contributor to the Architecture in Detail series and author of *Los Angeles Architecture*, also published by Phaidon.

Phaidon Press Limited
Regent's Wharf
All Saints Street
London N1 9PA

Twentieth-Century Houses first
published 1999
© 1999 Phaidon Press Limited
ISBN 0 7148 3870 5

A CIP catalogue record for this book is available
from the British Library.

Printed in Hong Kong

Fallingwater originally published in
Architecture in Detail series 1994
© 1994 Phaidon Press Limited
Villa Mairea originally published in
Architecture in Detail series 1992
© 1992 Phaidon Press Limited
Photography © 1992 Rauno Träskelin
and the Villa Mairea Foundation
Eames House originally published in
Architecture in Detail series 1994
© 1994 Phaidon Press Limited